Praise for *Guess What? I Love You*

"A memoir that speaks true to the overwhelming grief of a cherished time cut short, and to the joy of a richly remembered relationship."
— *Kirkus Reviews* • *Get it.*

"An honest, moving account of love, loss and the radical act of staying open to possibility."
— *Los Angeles Magazine*

"A heartfelt, poignant memoir… that expresses the author's profound thoughts about success, failed relationships, and self-worth. Most importantly, Mike and Howard are an exceedingly sympathetic couple, impossible not to root for. Readers looking for real-life examples of enduring, mature love standing firm against all challenges will fully enjoy *Guess What? I Love You*."
— *BlueInk Review* ★ Starred Review

"The book is a masterclass in emotional precision. It is an essential read for anyone navigating grief, proving that love's spectrum remains vast even in the face of loss."
— *The Fight Magazine*

"This release holds significance for the LGBTQ+ community, where grief from loss—whether by death or separation—intersects with broader resilience narratives. Maimone's emphasis on healing offers a model for transgender people, gay men, and others processing personal tragedies through art."
— *Edge Media Network*

"Guess what? I loved it! Mike Maimone's beautifully written, deeply moving memoir will stir the soul of anyone who reads it. This story captures all the joy, wonders, and heartaches of finding a new love, only to end tragically. Maimone brings vividly to life his improbable love story with Hollywood PR genius Howard Bragman. As a tribute, Maimone explains Howard's impact on the lives of a wide range of celebrities and incorporates historic changes that Bragman was involved in. But the heart of this book is the very moving private relationship of two men whose lives come together through the magic of love, in an extraordinary way that neither one thought was possible, showing us all that love can last a lifetime—even through death."

— THOMAS MAIER, New York Times bestselling author of *Masters of Sex*

"*Guess What? I Love You* depicts the heartfelt journey of two individual souls divinely threaded together by the mystical circumstances of life, and how they live out the rarest of human understandings of true love. Utilizing slices of charm and entertainment, this beautifully crafted piece demonstrates that love, in its purest form, lives beyond time and space and continues to grow stronger with the dawning of each new day!"

— JAMES VAN PRAAGH, #1 New York Times bestselling spiritual medium

"One of those understated revelations that says something big and elusive about what it means to be alive. About the beauty of loving someone. And the impossibility of losing them. It's writing that sticks with you.

Mike is a truly gifted writer. I particularly loved his voice; it's smart, funny, warm, and leaps off the page. From the early scenes of their growing bond to the tender unfolding of Howard's illness, I felt pulled entirely into their world. The way Mike captures their love – the intimacy, the playfulness, their resilience in the face of heartbreak and their insistence on loving each other despite it – is deeply moving. It is a powerful testament to their relationship, to who Howard was as a person, and to Mike's gifts as a writer who captures it all."

— CELESTE FINE, Park, Fine & Brower Literary Agency

GUESS WHAT?
I LOVE YOU

Albums by Mike Maimone:

Guess What? I Love You (2026)
Object Permanence XI (2024)
Unfollow EP (2024)
Songs for You, Alive in Chicago (2023)
The Studio Nashville EP (2023)
Borrowed Tunes, vol. 2: Songs for You (2023)
Mookie's Big Gay Mixtape (2023)
Broke, Not Broken (2021)
isolation:001 (2020)
Borrowed Tunes, vol. 1 (2020)
Stuck Together (Mutts, 2019)
Stick Together EP (Mutts, 2017)
Ghoul Yer Delusion EP (Mutts, 2015)
Fuel Yer Delusion, vol. 4 (Mutts, 2014)
Object Permanence (Mutts, 2013)
Separation Anxiety (Mutts, 2012)
Pray for Rain (Mutts, 2011)
The Tells of Parallels EP (Mutts, 2010)
We Float EP (Mutts, 2010)
Pretty Pictures EP (Mutts, 2009)
Open Mic Nights, Empty Bottle Mornings (2008)

These titles and more available on 8eat8 Records:

www.8eat8.com

GUESS WHAT?
I LOVE YOU

Mike Maimone

Fox & Quill
Los Angeles Nashville

FOX & QUILL
www.fox-quill.com

Copyright ©2026 by Mike Maimone

Fox & Quill supports the right to free expression and the value of copyright. The purpose of copyright is to encourage writers and artists to produce the creative works that enrich our culture. Thank you for buying an authorized copy of this book.

The scanning, uploading, and distribution of this book without permission is a theft of the author's intellectual property. If you would like permission to use material from the book (other than for review purposes), please contact permissions@fox-quill.com. Thank you for your support of the author's rights.

This book is a work of nonfiction, based on the author's recollections. While every effort has been made to portray events faithfully, some details may have been condensed and dialog reconstructed. Certain names have been changed to protect the privacy of individuals.

Fox & Quill
468 North Camden Drive, Second Floor
Beverly Hills, CA 90210

The publisher is not responsible for websites (or their content) that are not owned by the publisher.

The author is available for speaking events. Email speakers@fox-quill.com for information.

Jacket artwork by Vinnie Rico

ISBNs: 979-8-9935326-3-9 (hardcover) | 979-8-9935326-2-2 (paperback)
979-8-9935326-0-8 (ebook) | 979-8-9935326-1-5 (audiobook)
LCCN: 2025922363

First Edition: February 2026

Printed in the United States of America
10 9 8 7 6 5 4 3 2 1

*For Howard,
my forever guy.*

Track List

Introduction
1. Once in a Lifetime
2. A Song for You
3. Can't Get Enough
4. On My Way
5. Meet Me
6. Forever Again
7. Going to California
8. Paranoid in Paradise
9. Gonna Build a Mountain
10. Long Way Down
11. I Hate Everybody But You
12. Moon River
13. Put On a Happy Face
14. Via Chicago
15. Our House
16. Head Over Feet
17. Summertime
18. My Baby Loves Me
19. Flint City Shake It
20. Gimme Some
21. No Time at All
22. Right One
23. If You Want to Sing Out, Sing Out
24. Bosom Buddies
25. Something So Right
26. Guess What? I Love You
27. This Must Be the Place
28. I've Got My Love to Keep Me Warm
29. What Are You Doing New Year's Eve?
30. You've Got a Friend in Me
31. The Best
32. Beautiful Mess
33. Comeback Story
34. I Got You Babe
35. I Wish I Was the Moon
36. Helpless
37. I Live for You
38. Castles Made of Sand
39. I Think It's Going to Rain Today
40. Any Major Dude
41. Both Sides Now
42. Let It Be
43. Chapel of Love
44. Hallelujah
45. Waiting in the Light
46. Slip Slidin' Away
47. So Hard to Let Go
48. Living Without You
49. Over the Rainbow
50. I Just Don't Think I'll Ever Get Over You
51. Oh How Lucky
52. Through the Changes
53. God Bless the Child
54. Butterfly

Find this playlist to accompany your reading at mikemaimone.com

GUESS WHAT?
I LOVE YOU

Introduction

Who am I?

I'm forty-one, a musician, and a widower.

Once in a Lifetime

1

September 4, 2023. Flint, Michigan. I arrived at the cemetery early to have a moment alone at my husband's grave. I was kneeling. The shock of seeing his name—Howard Bragman—carved in granite had knocked me to the ground. My tears dripped into the dewy grass as I struggled for breath, hyperventilating. Trying to wake from the nightmare, I closed my eyes and pressed my forehead into the stone.

This was not here during Howard's funeral; the Jewish custom is to have a temporary placard at the burial. The family reconvenes one year later to unveil the permanent headstone—a ceremony symbolizing the passage from intense mourning into a more ongoing remembrance.

Like so much in my relationship with Howard, his unveiling came sooner than usual. I was back in less than seven months.

When I pulled my rental car into the empty parking lot, Diana Ross was singing, "Someday We'll Be Together." The tune lingered in my head as I knelt at Howard's grave. Slowly, my breath settled.

"Hi, honey," I sniffled. "I miss you so much."

To the left, I saw the resting place of his parents, Leonard and Myrna. To the right was an empty spot where my own story ends.

I knew this because only a few months after we'd met, Howard showed me his headstone design and said he'd bought two plots together. We had been planning our wedding already, and I advised him that we should talk more about spending our lives together before we discussed spending our deaths together.

But Howard's policy was to tackle the impossible issues head-on.

Howard Bragman was a bear of a man, standing six foot four and built like a defensive lineman. But he was a gentle giant; his clients regarded him as a guardian angel. He earned the nickname "The Gay Guru" for helping celebrities come out during less accepting times. This work increased visibility for the LGBTQ+ community, familiarizing the world with the personal journeys of Chaz Bono, Don Lemon, actors Meredith Baxter and Dick Sargent, professional basketball stars Sheryl Swoopes and John Amaechi, the first active and out NFL player Michael Sam, country music singers Chely Wright and Ty Herndon, and dozens more.

Gradually our culture became more accepting—due in part to Howard's own behind-the-scenes efforts—and Howard carved out a new professional niche. He used his "run-toward-the-fire" superpower to pioneer the crisis-management field of publicity.

He taught his expertise at USC and published a best-selling book on the topic. He became a celebrity in his own right, appearing on shows as varied as *Larry King Live*, *RuPaul's Drag Race*, *Good Morning America*, and *Pause with Sam Jay* to weigh in on the hot-button issues of the day. He was quoted in everything from TMZ to the BBC. When *Rolling Stone* cited him, I teased that I was the musician, yet he got into the iconic music magazine without even trying.

So of course, as a lauded publicist, it didn't seem outlandish that he'd control his own narrative all the way through his burial.

Although I worried that my husband-to-be had sketched out his own tombstone design, he assured me he was in good health and simply didn't want to leave this important last word up to chance.

I believe what he said was, "I don't want anyone to fuck it up."

Fair enough. But I pointed out an issue we needed to address. The epitaph he'd chosen was:

Two roads diverged in a wood, and I—
I took the one less traveled by.

In the original text, this line of the poem concludes with a comma.

"You can't turn the comma into a period," I said. "You'd be forever known as the guy who edited Robert Frost."

"That's true," Howard said slowly, rolling the idea around in his head. "But a comma doesn't seem right there."

"What about no punctuation mark at all?" I asked.

"Hmm," he said pensively.

He paused to visualize it. "Yeah, babe," he concluded. "That's it."

It made me proud whenever Howard sought my editing advice. He was a great writer; many journalists simply published his press releases rather than composing their own articles. I wanted to cover all the bases for him.

"Why not just finish the poem?" I asked.

"Shorter is better," Howard replied. "And I like the way it reads."

"Okay," I said, "then I'll finish it for us."

I used my thumbs and index fingers to block out my theoretical headstone in the air. "My epitaph will say, 'dot dot dot, and that has made all the difference.'"

The imagery brought tears to our eyes as we pictured our bond etched in stone. Things were moving so fast—but so naturally. I hadn't believed in soulmates before Howard. But he taught me the Yiddish word *bashert*, meaning "destined." It's often used to describe the person one is meant to be with. Finally, the concept clicked.

People throw those words around all the time. But it's the unspoken things that define them. When we met, I was about to turn forty-one, and Howard had just turned sixty-six. We had waited a long time for this kind of love—understood with just a meeting of our eyes. When we finally said, "Nice to meet you," our souls were saying, "What took you so long?"

Howard taught me many things about Judaism. But one I had to learn without him is how practiced Jews are at mourning.

During *Shiva*—the seven-day mourning period after the burial of a loved one—his family and friends kept me company, sharing food and stories. Together we celebrated Howard and his remarkable life.

The week after his funeral, I was surrounded by his loved ones. It didn't bring my husband back. But it was better than being alone.

Throughout the next month, they continued to check in on me regularly, helping me to feel an enduring connection with Howard. Each month thereafter, I lit a special *Yahrzeit* candle, which burned for one full day. I said a prayer for Howard and heard again from loved ones. After twelve months, we were to meet at the cemetery for the headstone unveiling ceremony.

But Howard's Aunt Barbara had passed away five months before he did. The family decided that since both relatives were buried in the same cemetery, it would be fitting to combine their ceremonies. It would also be better weather than returning to Flint in February.

They were right. It was a beautiful Labor Day morning, not a cloud in the sky. The sun was still at an angle that made everything soft and golden. And the moon hung vividly over the trees as if to pay its last respects, too. It looked so out of place, it just made sense.

At the hotel breakfast that morning, I'd heard the headline, "India becomes fourth nation to land on the moon," and reflexively thought, *Why?* But here it was, a crystal-clear, nearly full moon hanging above the tree line at 9:30 a.m., as if to say, *Why not? Nothing is normal now.*

My new family arrived. We greeted each other with hugs and handshakes. It was surreal. Howard and I had spent time together with his closest relatives, but I had only met most of his cousins, aunts, and uncles at his funeral. They still welcomed me as family. I felt slightly less alone during my first unveiling.

At the end of the ceremony, everyone recited a prayer called the *Mourner's Kaddish* in Hebrew. Everyone but me.

I got lost in the rhythm of unfamiliar words. I looked at the headstone with my husband's name on it. The sounds swirled around me. My vision blurred. I felt dizzy. *My husband.* My stomach churned. *My husband? Did that really happen?* My temples throbbed. *I don't have a wedding ring.* My eyes burned, so I shut them.

My mind wandered to music, as usual. David Byrne crept into my consciousness, and in his trademark talk-singing style said, "And you may ask yourself, well, how did I get here?"

I'd asked myself that question repeatedly as I drifted without Howard from one moment to the next for seven months.

I asked it while receiving marriage and death certificates on the same day; while sharing the stage with Stevie Wonder; while finding my name in *The New York Times* after the words "survived by"; and while reading a beautiful message from Oprah.

I asked it during meals with Howard's friends—without Howard.

I asked it while standing with my new in-laws at my husband's grave in Michigan.

And I asked it while flying back to the city where I suddenly lived.

The plane touched down in Los Angeles and snapped me back into reality. Not the one I wanted to be in, where Howard waited to meet me at home. But the alternate universe I'd entered, in which none of this was fathomable seven months and a day ago.

It's not like I expected Howard to be at the house when I got there. But maybe that's what did me in.

I dropped my bags inside the front door, worn out from the emotional journey. The familiar scent of this place confirmed the merciless truth: this was our home, but Howard wasn't here.

How could these two truths occupy the same space?

I locked the door behind me. "Honey, I'm home," I said softly.

I plodded up the stairs to our bedroom. Sun streamed through large windows. On Howard's nightstand sat a stuffed animal he'd given me for my birthday. It was a tiny brown ox.

"Get off me, you lummox!" Howard had giggled, my weight too much for him. It was early on; we hadn't dialed in our couch cuddle.

"I don't think that word means what you think it does," I said.

"Like a big, heavy ox," he said.

"No, I'm pretty sure it's like an ogre."

It became our thing. Together, we were a couple of "lummoxen."

I had put one of Howard's pairs of reading glasses on the tiny animal's nose. From its spot on his nightstand, the glasses reflected the windows just as they would when Howard sat in bed reading. The sight usually helped me rediscover my smile.

Except this time. The room was empty, and so was I. This time it just brought home how cruel it was that I had lost him—my forever guy. The only man I'd ever met who could make me feel completely at ease with nothing more than his presence.

When I picked up the stuffed animal, my chest tightened. "My lummox," I whispered. I adjusted the reading glasses. "My husband," I said. And with that, the tears came.

I rolled onto my side, clutching our silly little inside joke in my arms. My entire body heaved as I cried just as hard as I had the night Howard passed. I lost control of my senses and wailed audibly. My sides heaved as noises escaped, not from my throat, but from my broken heart. They could not be stifled; the cries were as involuntary as breath itself.

Nuzzling my little lummox against my forehead, I felt like the only soul on the planet, now that my soulmate was gone. I cried until exhausted. The sun went down, but I couldn't sleep.

Feeling numb, I drifted downstairs. I slipped a picture frame out of my suitcase and plopped down onto the couch. It was one of my favorite photos of Howard, professionally shot for a magazine article about renovating this home just before we met.

Back then, I was living in Nashville, working on my music career while making ends meet as a freelance web designer.

Not rich and famous but earning a living.

Enjoying life as a single man for the first time in thirteen years.

Unaware of Howard, who was unaware of me.

Now here I sat, in the very spot where this photo was taken.

Starting over in a new city, thousands of miles from my family, friends, and bandmates.

I shook my head in disbelief.

How did I get here?

A Song for You

I've been a touring "band dude" for seventeen years. How does one survive life in a van for so long? Not by sex, drugs, and rock 'n' roll. I've seen friends "make it," only to burn out on the clichéd vices of the industry. For me, longevity as a musician has meant being relatively boring: waking up, exercising, eating healthy food, and doing some work before the show.

If I had gone to the school of rock, my senior superlative would've been "Least Deserving of a Rockumentary."

Instead, I went to the University of Notre Dame and got a degree in accounting. I worked as an auditor for a year and then brought that practicality into my music career. Spending more of my adult life in dive bars than in my own apartment, my sustainable routine kept me pushing, making music for nearly two decades by the day my life changed forever.

February 26, 2022. Knoxville, Tennessee. I was having a perfectly normal morning—same schedule, different city. I awoke before the rest of my band and quietly slipped out of the room that the four of us shared. Along with singer, songwriter, videographer, producer, recording engineer, booking agent, accountant, paralegal, graphic artist, merchandiser, social media coordinator, advertiser, show promoter, and website designer of my band, I also wore the hat of tour manager. When booking our lodging, I opted for 2½-star hotels because they always had a workout room and free breakfast.

The gym at this hotel was one of the newly remodeled exercise rooms with motivational quotes stenciled on the walls next to framed stock photos and mirrors mounted in reclaimed wood. Sort of felt like working out on Pinterest. Afterward I headed to the hotel breakfast bar and filled my plate with omelet discs.

I skimmed *The New York Times* digest and then flipped over to Scruff while I ate. My hookup app of choice was just for looking on the road. Practically speaking, there was no privacy when spending all day in a van and sharing one hotel room at night. But also, sex without a meaningful connection always left me feeling empty.

I perused the grid of profile pics sorted by distance from me, but there was not much to look at in my immediate vicinity. Mostly guys with no photo (married and on the down low) or closeups of their chests (single but closeted).

Checking my DMs, I scrolled through the usual litany of inane one-word messages: "sup," "lookin?" and "hey" are the holy trinity of hookup app greetings.

But at the very bottom of my inbox—on an unpaid Scruff profile, you can only see the most recent ten chats—I was shocked to find a message naming two of my musical heroes:

> Love child of Leon Russell and Randy Newman?

My heart fluttered. Who was this guy? I noticed there were previous messages, so I scrolled up. Turns out we chatted briefly on February 24, two days earlier. I would later learn that it was Howard's birthday. Put a pin in that—we'll come back to it.

I revisited our initial exchange. It was the morning I left for this run of shows. Howard opened with:

> Sexy. Hey.

Ok, so just two words. Not an auspicious start, but at least he had a profile pic of his face. His smile leapt from the screen, and he had salt and pepper hair, with a tuft poking out of his shirt. He was my type, and handsome.

I saw that we had traded a few risqué photos and comments. It's the 2020s; you know how these things work.

And for me, that concluded our first interaction. I hopped in my tour van to pick up my band.

Thank God I checked in two days later, or that life-changing message would've been buried forever.

He had messaged me several times after I left:

> I'm Howard
>
> Hi.
>
> I've been needing a trip to Nashrock

Then there were more pictures showing his body in various degrees of undress. He had a content, confident vibe that showed he took care of himself—but not so obsessively that he missed out on enjoying life. And that big hairy chest of his took my breath away.

These unread messages concluded with several all in a row:

> Don't be shy, dimples.
>
> Mike?
>
> Too forward?
>
> It was beautiful while it lasted.
>
> No wonder country songs are all sad
>
> I listened to your music
>
> Very soulful
>
> Love child of Leon Russell and Randy Newman?

This was no ordinary Scruff chatter. He had cut to the core of how I saw myself as an artist. Along with his perceptive musical assessment, I was very much into his photos. Something about him felt familiar. Comfortable. I didn't want to mess this up.

I took a sip of my hotel coffee and messaged:

> Oh wow! Nailed it! Two of my favorites

The "typing" notification bounced onto the screen, and butterflies bounced around my stomach.

> I'd like to.
> Or vice versa

I could feel movement below the table. I looked around. Nobody was paying attention to me. I replied:

> Haha 😼😼
> Amazing pics.
> I find you very attractive

> I feel the same about you
> Cool energy

> Thank you.

The "typing" bubbles danced for a bit. Then stopped. Then began again. I waited with anticipation. Finally, he wrote:

> Let's go away somewhere

I paused. Vacation wasn't in my vocabulary. I had never even made time for trips with my previous long-term partners. Taking time out of my career didn't fit into my routine, so I stalled.

> We should chat first

But something moved me to revisit his profile. I reviewed his pictures. He looked genuine, classy, spirited, and very sexy.

I re-read his bio, this time under the lens of a potential meeting. He said he was an early-to-bed, early-to-rise type. He used "their/they're/there" correctly. Good signs. Hot, sensible, and smart. I let my guard down and decided to have some fun.

Howard sent his phone number. I got up and tucked my erection into my waistband like an eighth grader whose daydream had been interrupted by a call to the chalkboard. I nodded a quick "good morning" to my band as I slid past them and hit the button to go back up to our room and get ready.

In the elevator I took a deep breath, and then texted Howard:

> Mike Maimone

That was it. After a handful of Scruff messages we switched to texting and calling.

Moving outside of the app this quickly may not seem notable, but it's a bigger step forward than the lucky folks who coupled before dating apps may realize.

There are a lot of people out there who shouldn't be able to reach you at any time of day or in any state of mind. Many of these people hang out online. At least in the gay community, phone numbers often aren't exchanged until after bodily fluids are. Phone access is much more intimate than sex at this point in gay culture.

But I was taking a "Year of Yes." I was staying open to whatever the universe was sending my way. My look-before-you-leap routine was giving way to blind leaps of faith. Put a pin in that one, too. We'll come back to it.

I started the shower. Before I hopped in, I sent:

> FYI I'll be intermittent on texting bc I'm on the go today and drive the tour van

This turned out to be a lie. We texted back and forth the entire day. I hated endless text conversations even more than I despised long phone calls. But this felt different. It felt important.

We swapped birthdates and other basic personal information. Part of me expected him to ask for my social security number, at which point I would realize this dream was over, and my identity was in fact being stolen.

> I'm 25 years older than you Bucky
> That OK?
> I mean, I know I'm pretty

> I'm fine with it

> Good
> How old was last bf?

> 4 years older
> We were engaged, together 7 years
> Before that I was with a guy 20 years older for 6 years

I was texting from the driver's seat when my band hopped in the van. We had several hours to kill before the gig. Whenever we had free time, we would post up at a coffee shop and do some remote work. Everyone had their own way of making money from the road—playing original music certainly didn't keep the lights on back home.

We found a coffee shop with ample seating and Wi-Fi. It turned out to be attached to an evangelical church, which felt like a fitting place to sneak off and send Howard a real-time picture of my penis from a bathroom stall.

> Hmm. Catholic Scorpio football captain from Ohio. Who hasn't fallen in love with one of those before

> Haha
> Almost made the football team at Notre Dame...
> Tried out as a long snapper

"Almost made the team" was a stretch. Luckily, he continued:

> I went to Michigan

> No way

> Way

We chatted about our two schools and our Midwest origins. On the drive to the venue, I plugged my phone into the outlet in my tour van. It was nearly dead already from texting all day. I saw these messages come in:

> One question

> I'm not good at monogamy
> One man can have my heart
> But I like to share the other parts 😏 😈

> That align with you philosophically?

This question gave me pause. It was Day One of texting each other, and we were already discussing long-term compatibility. That aside, I had always been monogamous. It seemed rare in the gay community, but I liked being committed to one person.

When I was single, I enjoyed hooking up with couples. But I never envisioned myself on their side of the equation; it often seemed emotionally messy.

I preferred the simplicity of always making love to the same person—the one who would also be there to tackle challenges and celebrate victories. Loyalty felt more than comfortable; I found it sexy. When forced to be apart while touring, craving my person's touch made getting back together out-of-this-world electric.

My mind wandered. Those three-ways were pretty intense… What if it were possible to have that kind of sensory-overload fun, and then kick the third person out and fall asleep in the arms of the one I loved—instead of being the guy who goes to bed alone? That would be a new and different kind of loyalty for me.

But fear crept into that fantasy. I'd be hurt and angry if I found out my partner was hooking up without me. That sometimes became a source of contention for the couples I'd been with, when one would inevitably reach out to me without the other knowing.

I was behind the wheel, so we couldn't get into all of that. Besides, it was my Year of Yes—it was worth a try. I simply replied:

My band and I loaded our gear into the venue. Before each tour date, I used dry erase markers to write the show details on a van window and recorded a video of the doodle. It was a living show flyer, a way to document a life spent on the road. The alley behind the venue had some cool murals, so I stayed parked there to complete this pre-show ritual.

I left my phone plugged in while I filmed and then sat in the driver's seat with my phone charging while I edited and posted the video to my socials.

One hour until showtime. Being in a band consists of endless stretches of waiting, followed by intense bursts of hurrying. After a day of leisurely texting with Howard, I found myself overwhelmed with what needed to be done before our set. I had to move the van, find parking in downtown Knoxville, change into my show suit in the back of the van, run back to the venue, and get on stage.

I turned the key, and nothing.

Turned again… nothing. Not even a clicking sound.

I knew just enough about cars to know this wasn't good. I called AAA. Then, so as not to leave Howard hanging again, I said:

> Gotta run. Dead Battery. Crisis mode...

> AAA?
> You know, I handle crises for a living....

This was my first insight into Howard's remarkable life. But in that moment, I thought nothing of it.

> Yeah, they're here. Replacing battery

> I hate to ask, but do you have enough $$$ for the dead battery?

I only slightly took offense. Music was basically a break-even venture; it was my web design business that afforded me First-World luxuries like health insurance and my own apartment.

> I do. I'm not a rich man but I get by

> I don't care that you're not rich
> You're passionate

> I feel rich when the gigs are good and people are into it

AAA replaced the battery, and I hustled to park, change, and get on stage by our set time. Before starting, I sat at my keyboard and sent a selfie to Howard. He couldn't have known that this pic was more intimate than the nudes we had traded all day.

For the previous thirteen years I diligently sent these pre-show pics to my partner. The crowds ranged from a handful of people to a few thousand, depending on the gig. We dreamt of the day we would reminisce about our journey via these photos—perhaps from backstage at Red Rocks—and think about how far we had come.

But after six years, my first partner lost that dream. And at seven years, my second partner and fiancé stopped dreaming with me, too.

I get it. It's hard enough to be on a journey with someone whose passion takes the wheel. But it's downright irrational to expect this person to stay stuck in the back seat when the road takes completely insane twists and turns toward a destination that is not only uncertain but also unlikely to ever arrive.

After two failed attempts, I doubted that I could ever share my life with anyone. Despite our obvious immediate connection, I told Howard as much:

> And when we break up you can go all Taylor Swift and write a song trashing me

> Ha
>
> Well I'm not looking for a relationship, if that matters to you. I'm enjoying being single for the 1st time in 13 years
>
> 1st time as an out man, too

> I got divorced last year after 16 years
> Not in a rush. Having fun

There it was. After a full day of finding commonality and compatibility, trading sexy photos and telling each other how attracted we were, we put up a wall. This would be nothing serious. Just a little fun.

Any casual observer could've seen that we were bluffing.

What was it about Howard? We hadn't even spoken on the phone yet, but I wanted more. I welcomed him into a routine that was previously reserved for the man I thought I was going to marry.

We rocked the show and then drove back to Nashville. I could never sleep after a performance. I was amped up from pouring out my heart and soul on stage, from the fun of playing with my band, and from the flow of energy with the crowd. While the band snoozed, in my head I reviewed the set or worked on song lyrics.

I dropped off my band at their houses, unloaded my own gear, got in bed, and opened Howard's text thread.

A day's worth of pent-up sexual energy could not wait any longer. I sent one final naughty photo to Howard, checked out my favorites of him while I released the tension, and then turned out the lights.

I still couldn't sleep.

I grabbed my phone and looked up his Instagram. His most recent post was from his birthday two days prior. The caption read:

> I am overwhelmed by the calls, the texts, the posts and the birthday love that is being sent to me. I'll take getting old if it comes with this much love. Besides, it still beats the alternative. With love and gratitude, Howard.

I texted him:

> Love your most recent IG post
>
> I've been saying "beats the alternative" for years
>
> I think we're gonna find we have much in common. Looking forward to getting to know you.

And that is just what we did. We spoke on the phone the next morning, and every day after that—some days we dialed each other over a dozen times.

Despite our physical distance, our age difference, our clashing cultures, and our expressed desire to "just have fun," our lives intertwined immediately.

Looking back, I wish I would've gone further, faster. I could've dropped everything and moved to California. But who knew that before his next birthday, Howard Bragman would be gone?

Can't Get Enough

Our physical distance was our greatest challenge to overcome. After our first chat, Howard and I did calendar calisthenics, trying to bend our schedules to intersect. He respected how busy I was but lamented that I was unable to get away from Nashville for more than two days at a time. I had a residency playing every Wednesday night at a local bar, and my weekends were packed with gigs.

On March 2, five days into our phone-pal relationship, Howard told me he had a client playing a big show in New York City in May.

"Wait, what do you do again?" I asked.

"I'm a publicist," Howard replied.

"Ugh," I sighed.

"What?"

"I've never had a publicist I wanted to keep around very long," I said with a chuckle.

"Well," Howard said with a smile in his voice, "I don't do music PR, if that makes a difference. There's no money in it and I find it boring—tour press is so repetitive. I've been a crisis management specialist for a long time. Much more interesting work."

He suggested that we rendezvous for a weekend, catch a couple of shows, and see if the chemistry translated from the phone to real life. Incredibly, that weekend was open in my calendar. But I hesitated. We had been on the phone constantly for nearly a week. When you can't touch someone you're attracted to, it makes you want them even more intensely. It makes you take risks you ordinarily wouldn't take.

I reminded myself that I didn't actually know this man. What if I got to New York and he was a serial killer? Or had chronic bad breath? On Scruff, the first meeting was usually to orgasm with no expectation for further discussion. Three days in a hotel room with someone was a monumental commitment as a first meeting.

Then I thought about his client. He had been one of my favorite singer/songwriters—his first two albums were all over the soundtrack to my twenties. But it turned out he had a history of deeply problematic relationships with women and had recently been canceled. I worried that if Howard represented guys like this, what would it say about me for associating with him?

"So, where's your line?" I asked Howard.

"What line?" he replied.

"Like, would you represent Bill Cosby?"

"No," Howard said definitively. "If someone is clearly guilty and just wants me to help them weasel their way back into a career, I tell them I'm not the right man for the job."

"Okay, but what about this guy?"

"He fucked up," Howard said bluntly. "But I interviewed him, and I believe he really has changed. He got sober. He apologized."

I contemplated this.

"I don't know," I finally said. "Doesn't help when it takes getting called out for a celebrity to apologize."

"No, it doesn't," Howard said. "But on the other side of that coin, cancel culture freezes bad behavior in place. There's no room for people to improve, or to rebuild bridges. Once the court of public opinion has ruled, it's almost impossible to come back—and it's not always fair. So if I think someone deserves it, I help them get a shot at redemption. Doesn't mean we'll succeed. Ultimately, it's up to my client to follow through."

He sounded confident. I wasn't quite sure. I envisioned finally becoming a successful artist and then reports of my relationship with Howard Bragman getting me canceled by association.

Still, there were so many things that intrigued me about this man. And it would just be a weekend. This was my Year of Yes, so I agreed to take a chance and meet Howard in New York City.

The plan was in place, and we just had to wait.

For over two months.

We used just about every method of keeping in touch in the meantime. We talked, texted, and video called on WhatsApp. Separated by two time zones, together we watched movies and March Madness, helped each other pick out clothes, or simply left the line open so we could catch a glimpse of each other while we worked. His charisma radiated through the phone. We fell in love despite our distance—or perhaps because of it. We discovered everything about each other, warts and all, since all we could do was talk. My concern over whether we would get along for three days was replaced as my frustration grew that we couldn't touch.

Basing a relationship on sexual compatibility had not been a blueprint for long-term stability in my experience, anyway. There are two men who checked all my boxes on night one (feel free to re-read that using Carrie Bradshaw's suggestive voiceover). I unfortunately gave several years of my life before finally admitting that they weren't my forever guys.

When I told Howard that my "number" was probably around thirteen, he went silent.

"Like thirteen hundred?" he finally replied.

"What?!" I said, shocked. "No… I mean, I had one random hookup before my first relationship. But then I went from seeing one guy for about a year to a long-distance thing for a year, then I had a six-year monogamous partner, I was single for like a month and then I was engaged to a guy I was monogamous with for seven years."

Only breathing on the other end. It felt like I needed to say something else.

"I mean, since my engagement ended, I got on PrEP and I've been with maybe a dozen guys in the past nine months—so I guess I might be closer to twenty now."

Howard made a noise like a door creaking. I had no idea what that meant.

"Babe, is it gonna scare you off if I tell you my number is about a thousand times yours?"

"Whaaaat?" I said in falsetto. "You've got Wilt Chamberlain beat? No way."

"Oh babe," he said warmly. I wrapped myself in that word like a Sherpa-lined blanket. His tone was cozy. Despite the context it managed not to sound smug or dismissive. It was a veteran arm around my rookie shoulder.

"It's different for gay guys."

"I'm a gay guy," I replied.

"Are you?" he said with a laugh. He went on to tell me a lot of stories. Howard was open and unapologetic. Shockingly so.

I was quiet for a bit, pondering Howard's alternate sexual universe. I felt like I could trust him, because he flat out told me things that would've sent pre-Year-of-Yes Mike running.

"Not gonna lie," I finally said slowly. "That sounds disturbing and exciting at the same time."

Howard laughed. "Well, I can show you the ropes if you want, or not. But I think you'll find we do have the same morals."

I laughed. And then immediately felt bad. Like a knee-jerk that had kicked him in the balls.

"Sorry," I said. "I'm not judging you, I swear."

"Sure you are, babe," he said. It sounded like he was smiling. "But that's okay."

Over those first few weeks we compared notes on everything.

Growing up middle class in gritty Midwestern industrial towns. The importance we placed on family. Going the extra mile for our friends. Wolverines vs. Fighting Irish—we were football rivals, but at least we both hated the Buckeyes. We were spiritual but had grown disillusioned by the hypocrisy in our respective religious institutions.

And music. We loved the same music. I had never met someone as fluent in the Randy Newman songbook as Howard. He even knew more about current artists than I did. Age difference be damned; we could talk pop culture all day.

And perhaps most importantly, we both loved football. It's not unheard of, but it's not common in our community.

Howard disclosed that he'd had a crush on a football captain who was straight.

I was a football captain, who thought I was straight.

One of the walls I put up during this early long-distance period was telling Howard that I was "looking for a teammate to spend my life with, not a coach."

"I'll bet you had a thing for your coach, though," he said mischievously.

"Yeah," I admitted. "I don't know if it was self-preservation or what, but I never thought that way about my teammates."

I paused. I'd never told anyone the following.

"But we all used to weigh ourselves on the scale in the coaches' locker room. I'd hope to catch a glimpse of one of the coaches getting changed in there."

I felt a weight leave my shoulders, not unlike when I was thirty and finally told my parents that my "roommate" and I were dating.

I was a captain of my high school football team, and nobody knew I was gay—including me. When I saw certain men I thought, "hopefully my chest gets hairy like his," or "I want my beard to fill in that thick," or "I hope my hair turns gray the way his did."

I didn't realize that these were my sexual attractions. Self-preservation wouldn't allow me to believe that I wanted to touch those bodies. To kiss lips surrounded by a beard. I told myself that I was drawing the blueprint for my own adult appearance.

Howard was unfazed.

"So, you're an adult now. Why not just get yourself a coach?" he said. He made it sound so simple. I realize that he had his own best interest in mind, but once again, he made me feel understood, not judged.

We became best friends despite the differences on paper: born twenty-five years apart and living two thousand miles away from each other. We shared our deepest secrets and fears over the phone. Every morning we walked and talked for over an hour.

At any other time in my life, this situation would not have worked for me. I had two full-time jobs between music and web design, never finding time to simply go for a stroll to chat. And I couldn't talk during intense workouts of lifting weights or running.

But eight months before Howard came into my life, I had received doctor's orders to chill out and start walking.

I was diagnosed with pericarditis—the swelling of the lining around the heart—in June of 2021. When the symptoms first appeared, it felt like I was having a heart attack. I sat in the ER awaiting treatment, unable to catch my breath, with chest pain radiating through my shoulders, preparing to say my goodbyes.

Turns out one episode of pericarditis is not life-threatening, just extremely painful. But soon it became "recurrent pericarditis," which could very much become life-threatening. My cardiologist insisted that physical and mental stress both caused flares, which meant my entire lifestyle needed to change.

Pre-pericarditis Mike was decidedly *not* a walker.

But living-with-pericarditis Mike became a walker. The silver lining of my swollen heart lining was that Howard and I fell in love as we walked and talked.

On My Way

"Butterflies in my stomach like our very first night"

May 12, 2022. Nashville, Tennessee. I packed a bag for my trip to meet Howard in the Big Apple, called a Lyft, and headed to BNA.

As I sat at the gate, I took a moment to think about what was happening. Now that I was on my way to meet him, this Year of Yes idea suddenly induced panic. I was a man of routine. Calculated. Slow and steady. I didn't take leaps like hopping on a plane to rendezvous with a man I had never met. I pulled up the American Airlines app and looked at my boarding pass.

Group 1. Seat 1A. I was not used to this many 1s. When I got on the plane, I realized that he had gotten me a first-class ticket.

A flight attendant brought me a small white ceramic cup full of warm roasted almonds and asked if I wanted a drink before takeoff. I chuckled. "Sure," I said. "I'll have a coffee." The man to my right ordered champagne. I buckled my seat belt, noting the surprisingly ample amount of shoulder space. I could get used to not having to sit on an angle, jockey for armrest position, and type on my laptop with T-Rex arms.

The flight was comfortable and productive. I grabbed my carry-on from the overhead bin, made my way through the terminal, and down to ground transport.

Coming down the escalator, I saw a tall man in a black suit holding a sign with my name on it. "Mr. Maimone?" he asked, pronouncing my name correctly in a thick Irish accent.

"Yes?" I said.

"I'm Patrick; I'm your driver. Here, I'll take your bag."

Howard had sent a driver for me. He looked like Mike from *Breaking Bad*. The fixer's muscle. The one you didn't want to piss off.

Patrick set my tiny suitcase in the back of a shiny black Lincoln Navigator and opened the rear passenger door for me to get in.

I felt out of place in the luxury car. As we left the airport, paranoia gripped me.

What have I gotten myself into?

I pulled out my phone and Googled "Howard Bragman." I confirmed that the photos that came up matched the guy from our video calls. Even so, I was concerned that this could be some sort of high-level deception. I racked my brain for evidence that I was being catfished and abducted.

> In the car
> This is so nice, thank you.

> Patrick give you a hand job and a shot of whiskey?

> Haha no
> Water and mints though!

I looked up the address of the hotel—44 W. 44th Street. My basketball number was 44. Two 44s make 88, the number of keys on a piano. I took this as a sign and calmed down. Just as I hit "Directions" to find out how much longer, Howard texted:

> Where u at?

> 10 min out

We were on the same wavelength. I felt a little better.

> **Room 818**
> **Can come right up**

> **Sweet seeya soon!**

Room 818. Similar to 8eat8 Records, the record label I started. I was in mid-air on this leap of faith and looking for any sign of a safe landing below.

I was also starving.

> **You have any snacks?**

> **Maybe**
> **What you want?**

> **Cliff bar or whatever would do it**

> 😘
> **Forgot snacks for the plane**
> **Haven't eaten since breakfast**

> **All set**
> **You will want for nothing lover**

Patrick pulled up to a stately stone building on the south side of 44th Street. He handed me my suitcase, and I took in the façade of this classy-looking Midtown hotel. Towering stone pillars on either side of a giant wooden door. People bustling around in suits. The doorman welcomed me and reached to take my bag. The lobby was dark and swanky, with neo-gothic sculptures on the walls and dark hardwood floors.

This was not my usual 2½-star Priceline Deal of the Day.

I felt my heart sink to my stomach as the elevator ascended. Upon reaching the eighth floor, I double-checked the room number and headed left.

I walked down the narrow hallway, following a curve to the right and then a sharp left turn. My heart pounded furiously. I was having trouble getting a full breath.

I found room 818 and tried to breathe. I hoped I wasn't a letdown to Howard. Then I speculated that he might be a letdown to me. I wondered how tall he was in real life. He seemed tall from his pictures. I had never dated anyone shorter than me. Wait, were we dating?

My stomach growled. I reminded myself not to be hangry. I really hoped he had snacks in there. I knocked on the door.

It took him about thirty seconds to answer. He opened the door. He was taller than me by about three inches, freshly groomed, smiling, and as handsome as anticipated.

"What's your name? Are you my trick?" he said.

He sported an orange Polo shirt and gray gym shorts with the drawstring undone. If he was trying to play into my fantasy of hooking up with a coach on a team road trip, he was succeeding.

I paused.

"Trick?"

His smile vanished. Feigning disappointment, he rolled his eyes.

"You're bad at role playing." He opened the door wider so I could enter the room. "We'll work on that."

As I walked through the door, I let my roller bag go, reached my arms around him and pulled him close. He was real. I had my hands on him. Finally. I wondered if his body was melting under my touch as mine did under his. We lingered there for a second, arms around each other, faces an inch apart.

I closed my eyes, letting the warmth of his breath guide me, until I felt his lips on mine. After a long and slow kiss, our heads tilted to the side, our mouths opened, and our tongues touched. Months of anticipation for this moment made it feel as scintillating as my first kiss.

I gently took his face in both hands. My thumbs grazed the wiry hair of his goatee. I opened my eyes and pulled back so my mouth was just a centimeter from his. Our foreheads touching, I took a deep breath. This was really happening. And it was so… familiar.

"Hi," I said. It came out softly, short of breath.

"Hi," Howard said, sweetly.

"About those snacks."

He scoffed jovially, rolling his eyes, and motioned to the dark mahogany counter just inside the door. There was an assortment of munchies, including my favorite KIND Bar.

Mellow instrumental music played softly from a Bluetooth speaker across the room.

A king bed drew my attention, its white bedspread neatly in place. On it was a towel and a bottle of lube. The man knew what he wanted.

My stomach growled again. My eyes returned to the pile of snacks.

"Help yourself," Howard said, only partially making fun of me.

"Okay," I said with relief.

I bit off half of a KIND Bar and undid the buttons on his Polo shirt, pulling it over his head while chewing. He smiled at me, eyes twinkling. His chest was covered in salt and pepper hair. His olive skin was kissed by the early summer sun. I forgot my hunger. I tossed the rest of the bar on the counter, stooped down, picked him up, and laid him down on the bed. He looked at me, surprised.

"Nobody's ever picked me up before," he said.

"I'm pretty strong," I whispered, leaning over him.

"I see that," he replied, grinning.

A gentleman never discusses his bedroom activity. But yes—it happened, and it was, well… fast. What would you expect? We had waited nearly three months for this moment.

We showered together, then walked to a restaurant nearby for dinner. Two middle-aged men acting like seventh graders. Holding hands. Stealing kisses. Smiling like fools. That we'd only met in person moments ago was long forgotten.

Gay men of a certain age didn't get to have the puppy love that heterosexuals take for granted. We spent junior high and high school hiding behind masks. We stayed alone and tortured or confined our relationships to the shadows or tried to force ourselves to be straight. So as grown-ups, we melt and gush and do all the things that straight men got to do well before they had mortgages and man caves.

My mind was a blur. I couldn't believe this was really happening. I could tell he felt the same way, smiling mischievously across the table of a dimly lit steakhouse.

We returned to the hotel. Approaching the elevator, my cheeks ached from smiling so wide all night. As soon as the elevator doors closed, we pounced on each other, kissing passionately, pawing each other's bodies from head to toe. I untucked his shirt and reached my hand up to feel his chest hair. He grabbed my crotch. When the door dinged at the eighth floor we trotted to our room.

What followed was the sort of wildly disorienting sex that ends with everyone out of breath, covered in sweat, and facing different directions with limbs intertwined like a two-man game of Twister.

When I'd caught my breath, I got up to use the bathroom. Howard had unpacked his toiletries and it looked like he lived there. I picked up a cute little squat toothpaste bottle I'd never seen before. *Interesting*, I thought. *They make it so that it stands on its cap, but then the label is upside-down.*

I returned to find Howard had righted himself in bed, and was now wearing his reading glasses, scrolling something on his iPad. Smiling, I crossed the room and got in bed on the other side. I put my arm across his chest and pulled myself in close. Looking up at the glowing screen, I saw that the Scruff app was open. He was looking at guys in the area.

"Tired of me already?" I asked. I made my tone playful, but I was a little hurt, too. We'd had a magical several hours. What else could he possibly want?

"What do you think of this guy? Want him to come over and join us?" I looked. He was a lean, hairy guy, probably right between our ages.

I laughed out loud and climbed on top of him, straddling his lap and nudging his iPad to the side in the process.

"Howard, you're all that I need."

He looked a little surprised. Or maybe his eyes were just magnified through his glasses. Either way, he was the most adorable thing in the world.

"Aw babe," he said, putting the tablet down.

I considered it for a minute before saying, "I mean, at some point, sure. But I want to enjoy just the two of us for a while."

I laid on top of him, our furry chests pressed together. I could feel his heart beat next to mine.

"I'm so glad you're real," I said.

We made love slowly, sensually. There was less urgency than the first two times, more exploration. It was the difference between a rock band and a string quartet. Both are enjoyable. But adding some space between notes makes the melody linger a little longer. And the harmonies came effortlessly. We played the same chords at the same time. I had to remind myself that we were still on Night One.

Afterward, Howard drifted off to sleep on my chest.

I looked up and could see a faint reflection of our naked bodies in the polished wood proscenium above the bed. I'm not really sure what else to call it; the bed was recessed into the wall and there was a dark wooden frame all the way around. And in my mind, this king bed was like a stage for a performance. I'd never had sex three times within a few hours. Howard amplified the sexual side of me—at first over the phone and now in person—and it was exhilarating.

I looked closer at the reflection of the two of us. I liked how we looked together. I liked how it felt. In the hazy glow of our reflection—his body across mine, breathing gently while he slumbered—I was committed. I hoped Howard felt the same but feared that I had set an unrealistic expectation. Knowing his sexual past compared with mine, I'd come in like an underdog, motivated to play up to the more experienced competitor's level.

On Day Two, we woke up in each other's arms, having barely moved during the night. We started the day with our fourth orgasm.

"This is really not normal for me," I confessed afterward.

"Me either," he said. That made me feel more secure.

We ordered breakfast to go from the Red Flame Diner across the street and ate back in the room. Howard sat on the couch in orange sweat shorts and a white T-shirt, and I sat across from him on the edge of the bed, naked.

"You really like being naked, don't you?" he said.

I took another bite of my eggs and shrugged, smiling.

"Not that I'm complaining, babe, it's just interesting to me."

"Yeah, I guess I'm part naturist," I said, picking a piece of hash brown out of my thigh hair. Howard laughed when I ate it. "It just feels free, not wearing clothes."

"Not to me," Howard said. "I've never felt good about my body. I'm always struggling to lose weight and keep it off."

"Well, your body is incredible," I said. "And your skin is magic."

"Sure babe," he said, furrowing his brow dismissively. I didn't like his response. But I didn't say anything. I was still figuring out Howard's idiosyncrasies.

He took another bite of his bagel and cream cheese. "We gotta get going."

We held hands as we walked around the city. We told each other more about our past lives, past loves, our vulnerabilities, our families. This felt far more important than his client's concert, than meeting Howard's celebrity friends, and even more than eight orgasms in forty-eight hours.

We had waited long enough for this easy kind of love. And we dove right in.

In a blink, it was time for me to head back to Nashville. Howard walked with me down the block to where Patrick had parked, waiting to take me to the airport.

Howard shook his hand. "Hey Patrick, good to see you."

"Nice to see you Howard," Patrick replied. He took my suitcase and put it in the trunk. Traffic on Fifth Avenue whizzed past us. This needed to be quick.

Howard and I hugged.

"Best trick ever," he said with a broad smile.

"Come on," I sighed. "This was really incredible."

"It sure was," he said casually. "I'm growing quite fond of you."

He gave me a quick but deliberate kiss on the lips. I glanced to see if Patrick had noticed. He was holding the door for me. I climbed into the back seat.

"Let me know when you're home," Howard said as Patrick closed the door.

We pulled into traffic, and I looked back to wave to Howard. But he had already disappeared into the crowded sidewalk.

I was a little self-conscious that Patrick had seen us kiss. But it seemed like they knew each other. Maybe this was a regular thing. The paranoia from my arrival returned.

"So, does Howard send cars for guys often?" I asked. I didn't expect Patrick to rat on his client, but I watched his face in the rearview mirror for any signs of hesitation. There were none.

"No. This is the first time he's had me pick up someone that wasn't a client." His thick Irish accent seemed noble and trustworthy. I wanted to believe him.

I settled in for the ride. New York City felt like a movie montage out my window. The chaotic hustle seemed miles away as I pondered what had just happened.

My first thought, as usual, was an anxious one. This was my Year of Yes. A time to sow my wild oats, live it up, and go out with all kinds of guys. For a few months, I did. But I was already in love. Knowing that I'm a one-man kind of guy, was I selling myself short?

Meet Me

"Why don't you meet me in the Windy City?"

5

When I got home to Nashville, there was a package waiting for me with two books: *A Guide to Rational Living*, and *The Ethical Slut: A Practical Guide to Polyamory, Open Relationships & Other Adventures*. Howard must've sent this while we were together. The first had come up in conversation. The other I assumed was homework.

I asked when I would see him again to turn in my book report. Fourth of July weekend—six weeks away—was unfortunately the soonest I could visit him. The conversation turned serious:

> If you come to LA I'm going to fall in love
>
> Just telling you
>
> So happy to cancel now
>
> If I'm too old and you don't think it's ok
>
> I'll survive
>
> Because I'll be happy for the time we spent
>
> Sorry to be heavy
>
> But couldn't imagine wanting any more than you

Before I answered, I had concerns.

First, I couldn't yet reconcile that he wanted nothing more than me, with his opposition to monogamy. He had been on Scruff in the middle of our first night together. Clearly this is why he sent me *The Ethical Slut*. But did I want to read it?

Second, I worried that he was merely infatuated with someone just out of reach. I was starting to do well in Nashville and couldn't move to Los Angeles. Howard Bragman could have any man he wanted and there were tons of them in Tinseltown. This was fun now, but he would tire of a long-distance relationship eventually.

The transition from friends to lovers is thrilling and terrifying. I didn't want to risk losing my new best friend if we didn't work as a couple. I built the rest of my protective wall with bricks consisting of our age difference, our financial disparity, and our careers at completely different stages.

But now Howard's wall was down, and he was vulnerable. Out in the open. An urge to meet him there pushed my fear of our two broken hearts out of the way. I replied:

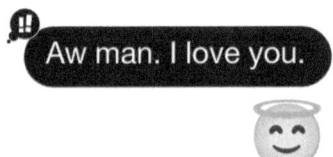

It was the first time either of us had mentioned those three magic words. He put the little exclamations on my text bubble, but didn't write it back. Maybe I rushed it. Maybe he drew it out of me. But no takebacks—I said the "L Word" first.

I told him I was definitely coming to L.A. for the Fourth of July. With hesitation I added that in the meantime I was fine with not being in a monogamous relationship.

Good news: We were officially "in a relationship."

Bad news: My first open permission slip would be put to the test sooner than I'd imagined. Howard was hosting one of his infamous "clothing-optional" pool parties a week after he returned from New York.

The morning of the party he texted me a photo. He had arranged hundreds of purple petals into a giant heart on his front walk. My favorite color.

I called to say that I missed him and asked when his guests would arrive. He intuited my reluctance about the event, saying that with everything he did, he thought of me.

"I'm sure you do," I said flatly. "Go have fun."

As I put down the phone, my heart sank. Maybe he could be surrounded by naked men and keep his hands to himself. Fortunately, I was able to distract my imagination from running wild by playing a wedding gig out of town.

The next morning, Howard called me.

"I did a bad thing," he said. I detected a mix of remorse and glee, but mostly the latter.

He went on to describe what happened at the party. My stomach knotted as he confirmed my instincts in detail.

I was hurt and couldn't hide my disappointment. I felt cast aside. When we hung up, neither of us sounded excited about the previous day's events.

Moments later, I considered what it took for Howard to tell me the truth. I let him know I appreciated it:

> Thanks for being honest with me I woke up lonely and now I don't feel as bad

> I feel worse lol

> But I will be honest because we deserve that

> No secrets

> It's clear to me that the party bothered you. I'm not going to do another one. You're too important to me. We're too important to me.

> I guess it did. Thank you.

> Of course.
> I like making you happy

> Don't change too much for me, love. Maybe I'll come around... 😈😈😈😈😈😈😈😈😈

June 2, 2022. A few days later I drove up to Chicago. I had a wedding gig, was producing an album for a client, and shooting a music video with my friend JC Brooks.

I called Howard from the road. Turns out he would be in Chicago the following weekend for a friend's wedding. I was invited but had to be back in Nashville for a gig.

"What if you came to Chicago early next week? I'll stay in town an extra few days so we can see each other again before the Fourth of July."

And with that, our second rendezvous was booked.

In the Windy City, we hung out with each other's friends. I met his Aunt Manya, whom he regarded like a sister because she was only a few years older than Howard. At every turn, we shattered social mores—from Scruff to phone calls on the first day, planning vacations in the first week, and merging each other's social circles on our second date.

As we walked around downtown Chicago, we held hands and talked about our drastically different experiences there.

When he lived there, he stayed in an upscale building downtown.

When I lived there, I chased affordable rent everywhere else.

He knew all the fancy restaurants.

I knew all the dive bars and music clubs.

"We have very different Chicagos," he said.

"Yeah, mine's the fun one," I replied, squeezing his hand.

Going our separate ways the second time was much more difficult than the first. But this time, and from then on, whenever we parted we knew we'd reunite in a few weeks or less.

Meet Me

    I left Chicago heading south for Nashville, when I got a text from Howard. It was a link to my song "Uncivilized," from my band Mutts' acoustic album. He was doing his research on me.

Forever Again

"Let's say it one last time"

6

Y ou can't overstate the importance of a partner who "gets" you.

As I returned to Tennessee in June 2022, I compared my life to the last time I drove my van from Chicago to Nashville.

Back then I was tailing an RV loaded with all my possessions, my then-fiancé Butch, and our dog. It was January 2020, and I had been engaged to Butch for three of the five years we were together. He was the first man I'd dated my own age, and we felt like a team.

My band Mutts had apparently reached our peak in Chicago, having fallen short of selling out our ten-year anniversary show. Four years prior we had been regulars on Chicago's many music festivals, sold out our shows, even headlined the Metro—a legendary theater whose storied history includes Nirvana, The Smashing Pumpkins, Pixies, Jeff Buckley, Fall Out Boy, and countless more. But we were heading in the opposite direction of those bands. It was time to shake things up. I was going solo.

Butch was from Chicago, lived there his entire life, and was also ready for a change. We decided to try Nashville.

I figured that we should tie the knot before we left, so we could party with our friends. I arranged for the marriage license appointment. But when I told Butch, he faltered.

He said he didn't want to take on responsibility for my credit card debt—another reason to put my band on hiatus was that it cost a ton to make and promote albums, but I was funding everything myself. My debt mounted with each radio and PR campaign.

And the publicists never delivered everything they promised.

I reminded Butch that I had paid all the rent for several months earlier in our relationship, while he went to graduate school. He was driving my car at that time as well.

Instead of heeding this red flag, I helped Butch put a down payment on an RV, sold everything we couldn't fit in it, and moved with him and our dog (his dog first, but I was Dad Two to our 140-pound lapdog) to Music City.

Two weeks after we moved, our dog died suddenly from a ruptured tumor. There were no warning signs. That morning, he was playing in the park. That night, I was at a gig and got a call from Butch. He said I needed to get to the emergency vet immediately.

When we left the vet without our beloved dog, we were in shock. It was the first time I felt like life had taken a wrong turn, and that our reality was somewhere on another road. If only we could get to it.

We couldn't stay in that little RV without our giant dog, so we rented a house. I was still getting set up in Nashville, and our financial overhead—with rent plus an RV payment—terrified me.

Then the pandemic hit and I canceled all of my shows.

Stuck with our grief in a new house in a new city, the cracks in our relationship burst wide open. He resented that I didn't contribute more to our household, I never planned any trips, and my career was stagnant. I defended myself by saying that we always used to do fun things surrounding my band, but live music had shut down. I resented that we stopped having sex. With all the alone time, I hoped we could reignite the spark. But he answered my advances with disgust.

We were in a downward spiral of circuitous arguments. We needed a reset. He took a three-month paid internship in a different city to give us space.

In his absence, I commandeered the living room with my audio and video equipment, making a quarantine album and accompanying short film. It was the most creative I had felt in years and revitalized both my spirits and my career. Even in lockdown, I was reaching new listeners. The film screened at a handful of festivals, and the record was my first solo project to get significant radio airplay.

Enjoying my new artistic freedom, I took the opportunity to try out a side project called SIRYESSIR. It was dark, sexy club music. For promotion, I posted sweaty after-workout photos on Instagram with clips of the song. The profile gained a following quickly. Messages flooded in asking me when I would start an OnlyFans—a subscription-based website that grew in notoriety during the pandemic as sex workers moved online to earn income.

I had the house to myself. Butch wasn't texting or calling, even though when I was on tour, the onus was on me to check in back home. I felt abandoned. Unloved. Yet here were men who said I was sexy and wanted to see more. It made me feel good.

I went for it. I set up an OnlyFans profile under SIRYESSIR and filmed my home workouts. My attire started out in gym gear and stripped down to boxer briefs as I worked up a sweat. For the last few exercises, I carefully set the camera to show I was nude without revealing everything.

If this took off, I would be making serious money. Stories about OnlyFans hit mainstream news. Many creators were earning six-figure incomes, while the most popular made millions. In that case, I'd find a way to explain it to Butch. He of course wouldn't approve. But if I paid off our RV he'd come around.

With my PG-13 content, revenue did not pour in. After two months I decided I'd shut it down before Butch returned.

Just after I'd made that promise to myself, I was reading in bed and heard Butch's text notification. A late-night message when he hadn't been in touch for weeks. Something had to be wrong.

I got out of bed and checked my phone. My heart sank. Butch had discovered my alter ego's profile on Instagram.

Forever Again

And then he found my OnlyFans.

I felt nauseous. I had betrayed my fiancé. We were on bad terms, but I never wanted to be that person to anyone.

When Butch came back from his internship, we tried therapy. He couldn't trust me, and I couldn't blame him. But I'd seen what creative freedom looked like, and I resented him for crushing it. I needed to explore my personal journey through my art, and that included my sexuality.

A crowd favorite at my shows was "Clear Black Night," containing the lyrics:

> *Of all the words I had*
> *I finally had to settle*
> *Has anyone ever told you*
> *you look like Burt Reynolds?*

People always laughed at that line. Butch was so irate when I first played him the recording that he cut it off before it finished. We argued for the rest of the night.

When I texted him the provocative video for "Dirty," a song on my quarantine album that humorously subverted the notion of homosexuals being unclean, he simply sent me the facepalm emoji.

I never bothered to show him "Taste U," a video comparing the communion wafer to the forbidden fruit of Genesis, since "practicing homosexuals" aren't permitted to take part in the sacraments.

When I reached this point in my comparison, I snapped back to the present and smiled. Howard absolutely loved "Taste U." The music, the message, and the sexy video. When it came out, he said:

> I love you being sexy. And sexual.
>
> You're hot. Flaunt it.

I turned onto my street, just past TriStar Medical Center, where I'd first been diagnosed with pericarditis one year earlier. June 2021. The chest pain had been so bad when laying back that I slept sitting straight up. This bothered Butch, so I moved to my studio to sleep. Eventually I spent all day there.

Butch and I called it off that month after nearly seven years together. I got my own apartment and helped Butch move his stuff into a storage unit. He was taking the RV and leaving Tennessee.

And then, while living alone, I ended up back in the hospital. The physical exhaustion from moving, working out, and performing, coupled with the mental stress of starting over brought on a pericarditis recurrence far more painful than the original episode.

Between the pandemic and this new heart condition, I pronounced my aspirations as an entertainer dead. I'd stick to the background, writing songs for other people.

Enter Howard Bragman.

When I returned to Nashville from our second rendezvous, it was June 2022. I was reflecting on how much my life had changed in the past year when Howard texted me:

> I forgot to tell you. Your movie is amazing. You produce, direct, act... you could be a star

He didn't say, "You're going to be a star." He said I "could" be.

Howard got it. Having succeeded in the entertainment industry himself, he'd seen it all.

He once told me, "You're talented and you work hard, but that doesn't mean you'll make it. You picked the hardest way to earn a living. It's been almost twenty years and you're still at it. Not many people stick around so long in this business. That's success."

I pushed back, "But I still design websites to pay the bills."

"You're looking at that part wrong," he urged. "You've built yourself a side business while following your passion. It's not a crutch, it's another success."

Howard's perspective restored my confidence. I got back to work with a new sense of purpose and optimism. His encouragement, grounded in real-life experience, was exactly what I needed.

Finally, a publicist who delivered.

Going to California

7

The next nineteen days flew by in a flurry of anticipatory texts and calls. I sent Howard photos from behind my keyboard before every show, including on the main stage of Nashville Pride. Howard showed me new shirts as he tried them on for my approval. We shared many sexy selfies. Life was humming again, but this buzz felt new and different. It seemed like this one was destined to last.

Soon I was packing up for my third adventure with Howard. We had rendezvoused in New York and Chicago. This time I was going to spend a week with him at his home in Los Angeles, culminating in an Independence Day party before driving to produce one of my client's new albums in San Diego.

I looked forward to taking our morning strolls in person, seeing where he had been all those hours we spent on the phone.

I called Howard to check in before heading to the airport.

He picked up and said, "Today's the day! I can't wait to smooch you!"

"Me too!" I replied.

"You can't wait to smooch yourself?!" he giggled. "You're such a weirdo."

I rolled my eyes. This was one of Howard's favorite jokes.

I was mostly excited, but slightly nervous. He told me there were two people in his life that I needed to impress. His Aunt Manya in Chicago was first, and I passed. The other was his housekeeper, Hilda. He referred to her as "The General," and I had to win her approval, or cohabitating with Howard would be awkward.

"I hope she likes sweets," I said. "I bought her fancy cookies from a local bakery."

Howard informed me that he had sent a car again. It felt superfluous, and I objected. I said I could call a Lyft, but he insisted.

Admittedly, I liked it when I saw the young man holding a sign with my name on it. Howard made me feel important.

The ride from LAX took about ninety minutes through heavy traffic. I was excited to see Howard in his element, although he seemed comfortable wherever he was.

We pulled into a roundabout in front of a dark brown building with no windows, only a garage door facing the street. Howard stood propping a large metal gate open. He wore a salmon T-shirt that said, "Not today, Satan."

I hopped out, grabbed my roller bag out of the trunk, and carried it across the small patch of grass.

"Do we tip?" I asked.

"No, it's included."

"Okay," I said. "Let me know what I owe you for the ride."

"I got it, silly," Howard said. The driver had pulled away. We kissed. I realized that I had missed the way his beard felt against mine.

"I missed you."

"Come on, mister," Howard said coolly. "I'll show you around."

Through the gate we entered a courtyard between two towering A-frame buildings of dark stained wood. Broad-leaved tropical plants looked like something out of *Jurassic Park*, while pine trees stretched high, covering the area in shade. It felt surprisingly cool for a July afternoon in Los Angeles.

His was the building on the right. An enormous bronze hand sculpture reached out of the front stoop, its index finger just below waist height. His street address was mounted in shiny gold numbers on the wall, and a Mezuzah hung at an angle on the door frame. I had butterflies in my stomach as we approached.

Howard opened the door and chaos ensued. I recognized his dogs from photos, but they did not recognize me. Nacho—a shaggy gray mutt—sprinted up first, yapping loudly. He kept his distance suspiciously, bouncing like a featherweight boxer looking for an opening. Curtis, on the other hand, strolled up with all the confidence of a terrier. He barked in response to Nacho but didn't seem concerned, sniffing my pant legs. I stooped down and petted him, which alarmed Nacho even more. I tried to pet him, too, but he took off running into the living room, barking all the way.

"He'll warm up to you," Howard said. "And when he jumps and hugs you around the waist, you'll know you're part of the pack."

We headed up the wide staircase to the bedroom.

We… well, you get it by now.

After working up a sweat, Howard slipped on shorts and a tank top to show me the rest of the house. I opted to cool off unclothed.

I noted that the guest bedroom bookshelf was lined with books, including six copies of *The Ethical Slut* and four copies of *A Guide to Rational Living*. Apparently, he thought everyone should read these, not just me. Only two copies of his own book, *Where's My 15 Minutes?*, remained.

We went back downstairs to his office.

"So, this is the couch where you sit when we're chatting?" I said, plopping down on a dark gray sofa with woven cushions.

"Yeah, if I'm not walking," said Howard, sitting behind his desk across from me.

I stood up, crossed the room, and put my hands on his shoulders. I kissed the top of his head.

"Awww," he sighed.

Next to his computer screen he had framed a selfie I'd sent him. I was shirtless, and my Notre Dame "Play Like a Champion Today" towel hanging in my bathroom was visible behind me.

"That's really sweet," I said, pointing at myself.

"My man never takes a bad photo," he said.

"I meant, my Wolverine put a Fighting Irish photo on his desk."

"Oh," he paused. "I didn't notice that part. I'll have to fix that."

Next to it was a photo of a butterfly. It looked like it was perched on a grilled cheese sandwich.

"What's that?" I asked.

"Do you remember what I told you about Myrna?"

Howard had told me about his mother over the phone. He came out to his parents after he graduated college in 1978 and started his career in Chicago. When he said, "I have something to tell you. I'm gay," his mother started to cry.

"Don't cry Mom," Howard told her. "I'm happy. I have friends. I have a good life."

His mother then said something extraordinary. Something that every LGBTQ+ kid would love to hear from their mother—but unfortunately most do not.

She said, "I'm crying for all the pain you must've had growing up that I couldn't help you with."

She was not only supportive of him from the moment he came out, but she also became a leader in her community for anyone with LGBTQ+ children who had questions and concerns. She joined Howard at rallies and marches, and if anyone told a gay joke in her presence, "she would cut their balls off," he said with a proud grin.

Picking up the photo from his desk, Howard told me that when his mother was in hospice and he was crying, she promised to let him know everything was alright by sending a butterfly.

"The morning after she passed," Howard said, "I was in a daze, eating breakfast on my patio." He swiveled in his chair to face me. "And then this butterfly landed on my toast."

I looked from his eyes to the photograph and back.

"And it stayed there," he continued. "It must've sat there for five minutes. I grabbed my camera and took a photo, and it didn't move." Howard knew that his mother had sent that butterfly to show him that she was okay.

I jumped as Howard's phone rang loudly, piercing the sentimental moment with the theme from *The Jetsons*. "Excuse me," he said, and answered the call. I slipped off to the bathroom.

Above the toilet hung what appeared to be a nicely framed crayon drawing of a young man with curly hair and a stubbly face smoking a one-hitter. At the top left was scrawled, "31.5.64 III" with a red squiggle underneath. I assumed this was from May of 1964, and that would've made Howard eight years old.

I finished up, washed my hands, and returned to Howard's office. He was off the phone.

"Honey, is that a self-portrait you drew above the toilet?"

"That's a Picasso, babe," Howard said, without a trace of condescension. "It's called *The Smoker*."

"Oh," I sheepishly replied. "I was wondering why you'd draw yourself smoking weed when you were a little kid."

My walls were adorned with tour screen prints, photos I took from the road, and colorful acoustic panels. Our very different worlds were colliding, and his felt far more sophisticated. I couldn't help but feel self-conscious.

That evening we took the dogs for a walk together. I held Nacho's leash, and Howard took Curtis. It was just as special as I'd imagined, walking in Howard's neighborhood, the place he'd been while we fell in love over the phone. Everything was new and interesting. The architecture was eclectic—some Spanish influence, some modern design, some that looked like the cottages back East. The streets were clean, and the sidewalks were lively with other neighborhood residents out for a stroll. There were a lot of hip-looking people. I could tell creatives lived here.

After a short time, we found ourselves along a wall obscured by tall hedges, more than a city block long.

"Guess who lived there," Howard said.

"No idea," I answered.

"That was Bob Hope's house."

"Oh cool."

"It has its own golf course and a gate house," Howard continued. "Guess how much?"

"Ten million," I guessed.

"Higher."

"Twenty million."

"Twenty-nine million," he said.

"Wow," I replied calmly, "That is a stupid amount of money for a house."

"Yeah babe," Howard said. "But after your first big hit record you can buy it for us."

"I don't think that's how the music industry works anymore," I said.

He would say something to that effect every time we passed Bob Hope's estate. I was going to write hit songs and buy us that house. I knew he was being cute. But I also knew that he believed in me. And that he saw us together in the future. I liked thinking about our future together, too.

The next morning, Hilda arrived. I introduced myself and gave her the box of cookies.

"I got these from a great bakery in Nashville," I said. "I'm sorry, they're a little smashed from the flight."

That night, Howard told me The General approved. I had passed the Hilda test, Aunt Manya liked me, and I was in the clear.

Or so I thought.

Paranoid in Paradise

"When he wakes up, I hope he likes the new me"

"If you hurt Howard, I'll kill you."

It was the Fourth of July. Howard had forty well-dressed guests milling about his house. Some sat eating and drinking at long tables by the pool. Others stood around chatting or admiring Howard's art collection and sipping cocktails. Caterers hustled around the kitchen. A bartender mixed drinks at the wet bar.

I was sweating. Previously I met his friends one or two at a time. This felt like being thrown in front of a firing squad. There were a lot of questions, although most of his guests graciously lobbed softballs.

Until I found myself standing next to the kitchen, with nobody familiar in sight. A man about my height, wearing a white button-down shirt and a scowl had cornered me.

"Excuse me?" I said, raising my eyebrows, surprised by the threat.

"Howard seems big and tough, but he has an enormous heart. If you do anything to hurt it, I will kill you."

His demeanor was intimidating, but it clearly came from love for his friend.

"Aw man," I said with a smile. "I think I like you."

The man's expression didn't break. He was dead serious.

"For real though," I stammered, looking around. No sign of Howard. This wasn't a candid camera situation.

"I love Howard so much," I said. "I would never do anything to hurt him. I want to protect him."

His expression softened slightly.

"Obviously, you are a friend of his?" I asked, feeling rattled.

"Jim Moret," he said, offering his hand.

"Mike Maimone," I said, accepting.

"I know," he said, squeezing my hand tightly, pulling me closer. "And I'm watching you."

He relinquished my hand. I looked to the kitchen, where the caterers were making noise, preparing dessert. It didn't seem like anyone had noticed what was happening.

I looked back, but Jim had vanished into the crowd.

Howard finally returned, arm-in-arm with an attractive woman who appeared to be about his age. I decided not to tell them about my recent brush with his bodyguard.

"Sweetheart, I want you to meet a dear friend of mine." I reached out my hand and the lady shook it. "This is Jeanne Phillips. She writes *Dear Abby*."

"What a pleasure to finally meet you," she said. She was dressed elegantly, with a black blouse and gold jewelry.

"Wow, it's great to meet you, too!" I said.

"I told you he was hot, right?!" Howard said to Jeanne with a grin.

She smiled and said, "Yes Howard, nice work." I could feel my face turning bright red.

"But he's a smart one, too."

"Oh yeah?"

"He went to this nice little *yeshiva*. You ever heard of it? It's called Notre Dame."

They laughed. Jeanne took pity on me.

"A yeshiva is a Jewish school," she informed me.

"Oh," I chuckled. I didn't know how to respond, but it was nice to be introduced that way. I felt out of my league around Howard's accomplished and famous friends. Despite the jokes, I was grateful that Howard wouldn't let the people he cared about assume I was just another hanger-on. His other favorite way to introduce me became, "I got lucky and found a hopeless romantic songwriter with an eight hundred credit score." He made sure his friends and family knew that I was financially independent so they would treat me as his equal, not his possession.

When the house had cleared, we sat on the patio together. I was exhausted from having just played twenty questions with forty of Howard's friends. He fielded reviews via text and relayed that I got passing marks all around.

Howard sipped an Arnold Palmer, his usual, and I had a can of ginger beer. This was how I'd imagined a beautiful California evening. The sun had just dipped out of sight, allowing the first few stars to poke through an indigo sky. The air had cooled enough to stop sweating, but not so much that I couldn't strip down to my underwear.

Howard pulled out a pre-rolled joint and a lighter. In New York and Chicago, he snacked on THC gummies. Now that we were in the comfort of his own home, he opted to smoke his marijuana.

"I get so paranoid on that stuff," I said wistfully as Howard took a drag.

"Yeah," Howard said, blowing an impressive cloud of smoke. "A lot of people say that."

"I know. But it's different with me," I insisted. "It's not like, 'Everyone knows I'm high,' or 'Do you guys all hate me?'" Howard chuckled.

"Everyone I've smoked with insists that I never do it around them again."

"Huh." Howard mused, taking another puff. He sounded intrigued.

"Well, if it's not for you..." Howard exhaled coolly, letting the thought trail off into another haze.

"I wish it were, though," I said. "Music sounds better stoned. And I can't drink anymore because of my heart. It'd be nice to have something help me chill the fuck out sometimes." Adding "the fuck" in between "chill out" emphasizes the need to chill.

We sat and listened to the evening. Distant traffic on the freeway hummed steadily. It was mesmerizing.

I thought about the situations in which I'd freaked out while high. Green rooms on tour. Parties at other people's houses. In each instance, I was surrounded by people I didn't know, and I had to find my way somewhere else to sleep.

But here was a controlled environment with a comfy bed just a flight of stairs away, and no strangers, only the man I loved. I wanted to share this moment with him. The music would surely sound sweeter.

"Okay," I said. "Let me try that."

"Sure, babe," Howard said, handing me his joint.

I inhaled slowly, cautiously... but once my lungs were full of smoke, I started to cough.

"Shit," I choked. "That's never a good sign."

I got up and went inside to the couch, knowing I was in for a rough night.

"You okay babe?" Howard followed me inside.

"I really hope so, but I doubt it." I could already sense that familiar feeling creeping in. It was fear of the fear. My mind was already spinning faster than I could logic my way out of.

Howard sat next to me on the couch.

"Let's just watch a movie."

He turned on a black-and-white movie, and we both sank into the couch. Within minutes, I started to feel like there were signs embedded in the film. Some sort of message coded into the scenes that I needed to decipher. It would inform me of the nature of existence. Obviously.

As I tried desperately to parse the information, then to remember why I was parsing information at all, I counted the number of actors on the screen. This was certainly part of the code. The scene was an elegant dance hall, with men in tuxedos and women in ball gowns. The camera panned from one end to the other, stopping on one lady in particular. She looked directly at me, trying to communicate something to me from the past, when the movie was filmed, knowing that at this exact time in the future, I would need to receive the knowledge.

"Howard?" I asked.

He didn't answer.

"Howard." I said.

No response.

I felt him staring at me. I looked over. He was staring at the TV.

I looked back at the movie. The woman had given up on me and gone back to her gala. I waited for another sign. But I could feel Howard's eyes on me. I quickly turned to him. He was still staring at the movie.

I took a deep breath. What time was it? *9 p.m.* My eyes widened. *It was 9 p.m. the last time I looked at the clock, and that had to be hours ago!*

"Howard!" I shouted.

"Yes babe?" he replied, calmly.

"Something's wrong."

"Nothing's wrong, dear," Howard replied without moving.

"Yes it is!" I shot upright.

Howard slowly stood up and moved next to me.

"Get away," I stammered.

"Why?" he said.

"I think… I've lived through this before," I said slowly, trying to decode the information that was coming to me in bits and pieces. "And eventually you have to kill me with that…"

I pointed to the dagger on the coffee table. Its ornate brass handle poked out from between two stacks of books.

Howard chuckled. "You mean this?"

He picked up the dagger.

It was a magnifying glass.

A round and non-stabby magnifying glass.

Not a dagger.

He laughed a hearty belly laugh. He was thoroughly entertained.

"Just go to sleep, babe," he said.

"I'm sorry, honey," I said suspiciously as I leaned back. Howard lifted a blanket into the air, but as it slowly floated down to cover me, panic again gripped me.

He's going to suffocate you!

"No!" I shouted and swatted the blanket to the side. I shot up and ran out of the room, up the stairs. Howard didn't follow.

I sat down on the bed to try and catch my thoughts, which were coming and going like six-digit authentication codes—forgotten as quickly as they arrived.

Howard suddenly appeared from the bathroom, startling me.

"Babe," he said, sounding mildly agitated. "Take this."

He held out his hand. Half of a yellow pill sat in his palm.

"No!" I said.

I smacked his hand. The pill went bouncing into the hallway.

"Well," he sighed, "now we have to find that. The dogs can't have Xanax."

"Nacho!" I whimpered, suddenly scared for the puppies. I dropped to my knees and combed the area rug until I found it.

"Now just swallow it," Howard said from a safe distance.

"Okay," I said, putting the pill in my pocket.

Howard climbed into bed.

"I'm over this, babe," he said as he pulled the covers over his shoulder. "I'll see you in the morning. And you're not smoking weed ever again."

I was embarrassed. I knew I just needed to sleep this off. I climbed into bed, my eyes drooping immediately. Seconds later, my paranoia alerted me, "This is what he WANTS you to do!"

A jolt of terror shot through me. My eyes popped open, but I couldn't move. He was reading my thoughts, hiding a screwdriver, lying in wait for me to drift off to sleep so he could stab my head with it. I was frozen with fear. "Just look over," the panic urged. "Turn your head!"

Finally, I made myself turn my head. Howard was curled up, facing away from me, breathing gently.

"He's faking," my paranoia insisted. "You've both stumbled upon the true nature of existence, he knows it, and he has to end you before anyone finds out."

I propped myself up on one elbow and leaned over Howard.

He was snoring.

I lay back down.

I guess he's not trying to kill me, I thought. *He's definitely asleep.*

I was totally wired. Waves of fear crashed over me, subsided, and then crashed again. I worried about what we are all doing here on Earth. I suspected that we each had to be reincarnated endlessly until we'd lived every possible triumph and tragedy, experienced the highest highs and lowest lows, and only then would we be able to move on to Whatever's Next.

Or maybe this is all actually hell, and there is nothing else. We are cosmically chained, sentenced to torment each other infinitely.

Howard slept soundly next to me as I stressed. I moved closer. His body's warmth was soothing.

Either I've been there, or I will be.

The phrase popped into my mind.

Reasoning with the paranoia, I proposed that if we do have to be everyone for all of time, then we have either done everything possible, or will do it eventually. The good, the bad, and the ugly. Therefore, how could we judge each other for anything? Shouldn't we just accept each other's differences and forgive each other's affronts? Maybe eventually, this all works out.

Either I've been there, or I will be.

I repeated it over and over until I drifted to sleep.

I had for the first time reasoned my way out of paranoia, using empathy.

Perhaps I was soaking up some vibrations from the man slumbering to my side. After all, empathy was Howard's most enduring trait, the superpower to which he attributed his success.

Gonna Build a Mountain

I learned most of what I know about Howard after his passing. In the wake of his absence, a wave of love washed over me, as his friends, family, former clients, and colleagues contacted me, sharing their personal stories. One word came up again and again: empathy.

Howard's personal journey began far from the bright lights of Hollywood. In the *It Gets Better* interview that I later discovered, he said he grew up "fat, Jewish, and gay in Flint, Michigan." It made him feel like "a Martian."

He spent a lot of time alone in his own mind while growing up, searching for his authentic self. That process, at times painful, gave him his superpower. He harnessed the empathy he learned through self-discovery to relate to anyone. He helped so many people through tough times that he was regularly sought after for guidance.

One day in particular stands out. This is one of those "music is in the space between the notes" kind of moments.

In the morning, as we walked the dogs together, Kareem Abdul-Jabbar's agent called Howard. Like many basketball fans, I was counting down the games as LeBron James neared the NBA's all-time scoring record. Kareem held this title for decades, but he would cede his top spot to LeBron soon. My jaw dropped as Howard turned down the opportunity to work with Kareem's team on a "passing the torch" publicity campaign.

"What the hell?!" I asked when he hung up the phone. "That's a piece of history you just passed up on!"

"They need a sports guy, babe. I recommended someone better for them." We kept walking.

Later that day, he got a call from someone working on the film *Emancipation* starring Will Smith. Howard turned down that job, too. He knew Black publicists who should work on this cinematic piece of Black history instead of him.

These were two perfect opportunities for Howard to tell me about the history he *had* been a part of—that he did PR for AIDS Project Los Angeles in the '90s, publicizing their important work for AIDS awareness and research; that he'd been a part of their legendary *Commitment to Life* galas, hobnobbing with the likes of Elizabeth Taylor, Elton John, Madonna, and more; that he'd visited the White House as a mouthpiece for gay rights and received a GLAAD award for his contributions to changing the narrative about the LGBTQ+ community in that pivotal era; that he'd met every living president (for better or worse); that he'd helped countless people—famous and otherwise—live their authentic lives with confidence.

But he did not.

Howard was so self-actualized that he didn't need to tell me about his accolades. He did things from altruism. In a society where everyone puts their merits on display for the world to see, Howard didn't need to brag. Pun intended. His name is "Brag Man." He was born to be a publicist.

When he started his own PR company in 1989, Howard knew he needed to attract the kind of mainstream clients who would keep his bills paid while he did pro bono work for the causes close to his heart. His mentors at his previous firm said he was crazy—this was the middle of the AIDS epidemic, and no brands would associate with someone who represented gays and lesbians openly.

This concept may be foreign to young readers. But for context, the first ad featuring a same-sex couple in the US was in 1994. It was run by IKEA, whose stores subsequently suffered protests and bomb threats. That quickly ended queer visibility in corporate America.

In the late 1990s and 2000s, the most progressive brands would covertly hint at same-sex couples in their ads. But it was always coded so that queer viewers would get the message, while leaving it ambiguous to straight audiences. It wasn't until a 2013 ad for Amazon's Kindle Paperwhite—in which a man refers to his husband, although we don't see them together—that a major brand dared to air a commercial featuring a same-sex couple.

Today, with marriage equality legal and more LGBTQ+ representation in media, we continue our fight for progress while standing on the shoulders of giants. Howard is one such titan. Directly and indirectly, he improved the lives of millions.

His legacy endures through the Howard Bragman Coming Out Fund at the University of Michigan. The university's Spectrum Center—the first organization of its kind, founded in 1971—continues to lead the way for on-campus LGBTQ+ centers around the country.

Howard helped forge the path that queer celebrities now walk on their coming-out journeys. His work with Chaz Bono, for example, made Chaz's public transition a source of visibility and courage—paving the way for trans people like Caitlyn Jenner and Elliot Page.

His life's work also resonates in communities where people feel empowered to live authentically.

Between 1989 and 2023, Howard built three successful PR firms that represented top brands and A-list celebrities while also increasing LGBTQ+ visibility and amplifying marginalized voices.

He never went back to his mentor and said, "I told you so."

Long Way Down

"It's a long, long, long... a long way down."

10

July 31, 2022. Newark, New Jersey. Howard and I spent most of the month in our respective cities lamenting our busy schedules. Both of our lives had flipped upside down. For the first time, work was no longer our focus—it just felt like the thing we needed to get out of the way while counting down the days until our next meeting.

Our fourth "honeymoon," as we had begun calling them, would be in the Hamptons. I had never been. Howard's friends offered their seven-bedroom mansion to him and his guests while they were out of town. Although I was intrigued to see what the famed vacation destination was all about, I had a hard time saying, "the Hamptons" to my friends. It sounded so pretentious.

Chaos surrounded me as I waited alone at Newark Liberty International Airport. The rumble of the baggage claims, the chatter of travelers searching for ground transportation, garbled announcements over the loudspeaker, periodic unintelligible shouting. My pulse quickened while watching luggage drop into the suitcase carousel. This always felt like a carnival game where the prize was just my own stuff.

I was exhausted, and my nerves were frayed. I had to put in a lot of work to keep the bills paid, and now I was cramming it all in between our adventures.

The night before, I had a wedding gig in Memphis. We got back to Nashville around 4 a.m., and I managed only a couple of hours' rest before heading to the airport. Waiting at the baggage claim in a mental haze, anxiety began to creep in. This would be our longest time together—eleven days. What the hell were we going to do in the Hamptons? I assumed people there spent most of their time counting money.

I knew I'd be critical of all the Rich People Stuff and feared that Howard would think I was ungrateful to his friends. I then started to wonder if the physical spark would remain after spending more than a week together. I took a deep breath and wondered if this was what a Year of Yes was supposed to feel like.

My small roller-bag arrived, and I casually retrieved it. Prize attained: my own clothes.

I went to check the board for Howard's flight. As I scanned for arrivals from L.A., my phone chirped his custom text tone.

> Landed
> Taxiing

> Sweet
> You are baggage claim #6

> You are soulmate #1

He texted me a link. It was an article about "Hamptons Bladder." Apparently rich New Yorkers were getting some kind of ludicrous Botox procedure to prevent bathroom breaks during the long traffic jam out to their weekend getaways. I shook my head.

> 👍 Rich people with too much money

The little thumbs-up meant he agreed. I was relieved. He could hang with the 1%, but he was still a Flint boy at heart.

Then a thought struck me. Were we about to spend eleven days with people who had "Botoxed bladders"? Would our longest trip together unravel our magical five months just because I couldn't handle being around a snooty Hamptons crowd?

I looked up the route to the rental car counter as I waited. It dawned on me that we'd never driven together. Traffic tells you a lot about a person. This would be a very telling trip for our future together.

Finally, mercifully, I saw him. The sight quieted my sleep-deprived spiral. His head stood out above the crowd, eyes squinting slightly as he scanned the signs for directions. He held the strap of a small leather carry-on bag slung over one shoulder as he sauntered through the baggage claim. I trotted over to greet him, my roller bag in tow.

"My man," he said in his low, gruff voice.

"Hi mister," I sighed, going in for a hug. By our driver's licenses he was only a couple inches taller than me, but it felt like I disappeared into his arms as he wrapped them around my shoulders. I squeezed tight around his torso and planted a kiss on his jawbone.

"Heyyyyy!" he said playfully, his voice suddenly an octave higher. "Wait, are you a homo?"

"Yes," I said. "Yes, I am." I kissed him on the lips as travelers streamed by on either side of us.

"Someone might see us!" he squealed with faux concern.

We waited for his luggage. The first one out was a large navy-blue roller bag with a bright orange tag. It slid down the ramp onto the moving carousel.

"That's mine," he said. I eased through an opening in the crowd and hefted the large suitcase as it passed. The orange tag said "PRIORITY," in big, bold letters.

"Oooh, fancy!" I exclaimed, setting the bag down between us. "Very nice, mister."

Howard smiled and feigned offense. "Yeah, babe. I'm so fancy."

I grabbed the handle of my suitcase.

"Hold on, grab that one too."

I turned to see a matching navy suitcase approaching us. I hefted it onto the ground. It was even bigger than the first.

"That's a lot of stuff for just a week," I teased.

"Eleven days," he clarified. "And I like to be comfortable."

I began to lead the way toward the rental car area. My stomach growled, reminding me that I hadn't eaten anything all day. The fog in my brain reminded me that I had gotten less than four hours of sleep.

Across the baggage claim I spotted a Dunkin'. I told Howard I needed a minute.

"Of course, babe," he said.

"You need anything?"

"I'm good."

I left Howard with our bags and zigzagged through the airport crowd. As soon as I departed, the timer in the back of my head started. I needed to return as quickly as possible. But as I joined the end of the line I looked back and saw that Howard already had his AirPods in and was immersed in conversation. I smiled.

It was a pleasant sight. In my previous relationship, I was always on the clock. Any wait would leave me with a grouchy partner for several hours. I was learning that Howard was like me—never lacking for something to do. In fact, we were both grateful for a quick opportunity to tend to one of the many irons we kept in the fire.

Returning with a large black coffee and small bag of donut holes, I raised a lumpy glazed sphere to Howard's mouth. Wrapping up his phone call, he shook his head to decline the snack. I took the bite instead. Then I tossed the rest of the donut holes in the trash can next to our bags.

"Didn't think so," Howard said.

"Stale. And the glaze is gross."

"I'd rather have some of your glaze," he said with a devious grin. Holding his backpack strap in one hand, he grabbed the handles of his giant and more-giant roller bags with the other.

I offered to take a suitcase for him, but he assured me that he was capable.

We approached the escalator down to the rental car area.

"You sure you got all that?" I asked.

Howard, leaning slightly to keep his backpack on one shoulder, ignored me and rolled his size-XXL suitcase ahead onto the escalator. He then followed, dragging his size-XL suitcase behind. As the step in front of him descended, half of his front case caught on the step on which he stood, tilting the massive luggage forward, away from him, and down.

My eyes widened. I had my suitcase in one hand, coffee in the other, and was out of position to help.

I felt my heart leaping out of my throat and my stomach retreating in the other direction.

Howard reached forward to keep the XXL bag from falling all the way down the escalator. But the XL bag behind him was now bearing down, having just caught on the step behind it. As the bag in front pulled, the bag behind pushed, and he lost his balance, his backpack slipping from his shoulder and spinning him around to face me, his back toward the plummet below.

"Howard!" I shouted helplessly, panicking.

In one sweeping motion, Howard whirled the rest of the way around, backpack swinging perilously, rolled his giant bag two steps below as he found his balance on the next step down, and allowed his slightly-less-giant bag to come to rest on the step above.

"Got it, babe." He smiled up at me. The move was as graceful as a baby deer taking its first steps.

"Oh my God," I said, my eyes as wide as ambulance headlights.

"Oh my God!" I repeated, looking at the distance we had yet to descend.

There were two people in front of us near the bottom. Neither of them would've been close enough or large enough to break Howard's fall.

The worst-case scenario played in my mind. In my mercilessly vivid imagination, I saw Howard tumble down a thousand feet of escalator.

My temples throbbed with stress as we slowly and peacefully descended the rest of the escalator. Howard was smiling.

"Never again," I said, shaking my head. "From now on, I'm taking your bags."

"Yes, babe," Howard said, chuckling.

"What?!" I demanded, brimming with anxiety.

"You looove me," he teased, with melodic emphasis on the word "love."

"Of course I love you!" I grabbed his enormous bags in one hand, coffee in the other, leaving him to wheel my little carry-on.

Howard chuckled. "My big strong man."

I Hate Everybody But You

"We got our own two-person parade, everyone else gets in the way"

11

Five hours later we got off at the freeway exit for Southampton, our energy dwindling. The first few hours of the drive had breezed by. Howard was either on his phone or we chatted leisurely while I drove and picked the music. Leaving New York City I selected soothing songs by Cat Stevens, Nina Simone, Stevie Wonder, and Sammy Davis, Jr. Once we hit more open highway I transitioned to Leon Russell, Randy Newman, and even added some Steely Dan for Howard (I still couldn't figure out why anyone would intentionally listen to that band).

But as our long travel day wore on, I started to fade. The lack of sleep caught up with me. I flipped over to Oingo Boingo. "Nasty Habits" was one of my go-to songs for staying awake. I didn't know if Howard knew them, but I was sure he'd know their singer/songwriter Danny Elfman. And the lyrical content was sure to entertain him.

"Babe, can you please put on something a little less thumpa thumpa?"

I looked over, expecting one of his usual mischievous smiles. But he wasn't looking at me. He was looking at his phone, rubbing his temples with his right thumb and middle finger.

"It's Oingo Boingo," I said, as if that answered his request.

"Okay, but my head is pounding."

I was annoyed that he was annoyed. I was playing chauffeur on very little sleep and ready to pass out. I was hangry, too. But I got it. Oingo Boingo is an acquired taste. I switched back to Stevie.

When we were a few turns away, Howard turned off his GPS. He guided me down a narrow, unpainted street with high hedgerows on either side. Every few hundred feet was a driveway, with stately gates of brick and solid wood or wrought iron. Through the gaps I could see that these hedges were hiding mansions. I'd been in big houses before. This was not that. We were in *Lifestyles of the Rich and Famous* territory. My inner monologue turned into Robin Leach.

We pulled into a long driveway ending in a cul-de-sac. Relieved to finally reach our destination, I got out of the car and stretched. We carried our bags up the front steps of the palatial estate. The door was unlocked.

"Hello?" Howard shouted as we entered.

A man wearing a brightly colored Speedo carried two champagne flutes on the far side of the house. We were theoretically in the same room, although perhaps our section was the antechamber and his was the main hall, with enormous paintings, wooden statues, and a concert grand piano. However you *HGTV* it, he was so far away I could barely make out his facial features.

He shouted, "Hi!" and promptly exited through a section of glass wall about forty feet tall. On the other side I could see a pool deck with several other men in skimpy bathing attire.

"Is that your friend?" I asked Howard.

"No, they're in London right now. These must be other friends of theirs."

Turns out, the house was occupied by eight young, lean, gay men. There was barely an ounce of body fat between them, and they didn't bother to notice the two middle-aged men with beards, bellies, and bald spots who had just arrived.

Suddenly, we went from a two-person parade to bystanders.

Or at least, I felt like a bystander.

Howard saw these young men and popped right back to life. After we put our bags in our room, he made himself at home in the kitchen, helping a couple of the other guests prepare dinner. I would've preferred a nap, but Howard had been rejuvenated by this group of physically fit young men.

We had just arrived in the Hamptons, and I was already feeling very inadequate.

At dinner, Howard passed around a vape. As everyone at the table but me got high, he told the story of my paranoia. He was a masterful storyteller. Unfortunately, in this case, it generated a lot of laughter at my expense. I didn't know these boys and neither did Howard. It didn't feel good that my best friend was sharing such a personal story with them. I was no longer grouchy-but-trying. I was hurt-and-over-it.

I remained as pleasant as possible until after dessert—I like to eat; I'm not just going to walk away from perfectly good food—and then I excused myself from the table. Our room was just off the patio. I closed the sliding door behind me and crawled into bed feeling very out of place and alone.

Howard followed moments later and stood next to me.

"I did something," he said softly. Remorsefully. It wasn't a question.

I explained the ways in which I felt insignificant. Not young, fit, or gay enough, not rich enough, either. And I said I felt betrayed and embarrassed by his storytelling.

I expected a defense. Some reason why I was being too sensitive. Or worse, an accusation that I'd misread his intentions and abandoned him somehow.

But to my surprise, he apologized immediately, without a trace of defensiveness.

The tension in my shoulders relaxed. He sat next to me, rubbing my thigh through the blanket. He said he was sorry again.

"I feel better," I told him. "Go have fun with the boys."

He was only gone a few minutes before he returned and got into bed with me.

"I just helped clean up the dishes. It's been a long day, boo. Let's get some sleep."

It was a queen bed, and we cozied up to each other. Howard fell asleep before I did, breathing softly in the little spoon position. With my arms around my big bear, I felt empowered knowing he was choosing to be with his balding forty-year-old over the brunch of swimwear models.

Not a typo. A group of gay men is a "brunch."

When I opened my eyes next, sunlight was streaming in through the floor-to-ceiling glass wall, and Howard was holding a small white coffee cup on a saucer.

"Rise and shine," he said with a grin. "You need to adjust to East Coast time. You're usually asleep until 10 a.m. here."

"And somehow you're still up by 8 a.m. here," I said groggily, double-checking my math as I swung my legs around and sat up on the edge of the bed.

"I'm sorry I overshared last night," he said as he handed me the coffee.

"That's okay," I replied. "I'm sorry I was so moody last night. I usually have thicker skin. I just have some work I gotta do this week, and I got the feeling that those guys' idea of work was putting on suntan lotion."

Howard rolled his eyes. "Well, now you're just being judgy. They actually left early this morning to get back to the city."

"Oh," I said, feeling like I had overstepped. Then I remembered a conversation in the kitchen. "But the one guy definitely told you he wanted a daddy so that his only decision would be which Speedo to wear in the morning."

Howard laughed. "Oh yeah, like *that* was gonna happen."

"He did look like an Abercrombie model."

Howard sat down next to me on the bed while I sipped my coffee. "I don't need a 'yes daddy.' I need a real man. I'm glad you're busy doing your own thing. It makes it more meaningful when we get together."

"Yeah," I said. "I guess."

"And if that was 'moody' for you, we're gonna be fine. Just come on out and relax in the hot tub. You don't have to put on a suit. Nobody's here and the neighbors can't see."

"You know," I said, feeling better, "I've never had hot tub sex."

"Let's fix that," Howard said. He took off his Speedo and I followed him outside.

After we dried off, I scrambled some eggs and toasted a couple of bagels while Howard sat on a couch across the living room. He had put on maroon briefs. I kept an eye on him while he answered emails on his iPad. He wore less and less clothing the more we hung around together, and I enjoyed it.

Sunlight poured in through large windows, casting half of his body in shadow, the other in golden sunlight. Artists swear that the light in the Hamptons makes everything more beautiful. Some photographers say it's a golden hour that never ends. I believed it; Howard was radiant. The contrast brought out the sinew in his muscly shoulders and chest, added sparkle to his salt and pepper hair, and chiseled his facial features, which were taut with concentration. I snapped a few photos.

I crossed the great room and sat next to him on the couch, our bare thighs touching. I put my arm around him as he swiped on his iPad. His shoulders felt warm. I put my phone in between his tablet and face.

"Look at you," I directed. "You're gorgeous!"

"You need a dog," he replied without taking his eyes off his iPad. He seemed to look through my phone and continued to work.

"What do you mean?" I asked, puzzled.

"Like a seeing eye dog, babe."

I kissed the side of his head. "You're the most beautiful man ever made, mister."

"It's okay, Stevie has done fine for himself and he's blind." He still didn't look up. I went back to fixing breakfast. "When we get home let's get your eyes checked."

Moon River

12

That afternoon, just as we finished watching *Breakfast at Tiffany's*, Howard's friends began to arrive. None of them seemed the type to have "Botoxed bladders."

When the movie ended, Howard asked if I cared to entertain. I sat down at the immaculate Steinway piano and pulled up the chords to "Moon River" on my phone.

"I didn't realize this song was from that movie," I told Howard, who was standing next to me. "It's so beautiful."

I started to play, slowly coaxing my fingers into the correct shapes over the keys. With minimal effort, the instrument sounded positively regal. Soon I had a simple arrangement, with sparse chords filling the great room. I looked to the lyrics for verse one.

Before I could start, Howard began to sing.

"Moon... river... wider than a mile."

I looked up in surprise. I'd never heard him sing before. His voice delighted me—perfectly imperfect, bouncing with charm. The song has a difficult melody, but he was getting it close enough. He didn't hold out the notes; he let them go as soon as he created them, almost spoke them.

"I'm... cross-sing you... in style... some-day."

He put one hand on my shoulder and the other on the grand piano, reading the words from my phone. I followed along and laid down the chords for him.

We slowly made our way through verse one. I paused a couple of times to figure out the jazzier chords. Howard waited patiently and picked up when I was ready. We started the next verse:

"Two… drif-ters… off, to see, the world…"

I had never felt more in tune with another human being. We'd taken forty-one and sixty-six years to find each other, yet here we were, finally drifting together.

"Moon… river… and, me."

I wiped tears from my eyes. Of all the festival stages and legendary venues I've gotten to play, this was my favorite musical performance.

I assumed it would be the first of many songs we'd play together. It turned out to be the one and only.

Put On a Happy Face

13

We went for a walk the next morning beneath a clear blue sky. I admired the hedges, all neatly trimmed, about twelve feet in height. More impressive to me than these wealthy homeowners were their landscapers.

This was an entire city of Bob Hope estates. Howard refrained from his usual joke about my hit records being able to afford us one of these. Either there was a limit to his imagination, or he sensed I was feeling inadequate.

I spotted a tennis ball in a gutter, its bright green fuzz matted with dirt. I kicked it gently ahead. It bounced off the curb toward Howard, who gave it a gentle tap with the inside of his toe.

"I'm sorry I'm so insecure sometimes," I said, nudging the ball forward a second time. It rolled slowly ahead.

"What do you mean, sweet angel?" Howard said. We took two more steps, and his left toe made contact with the neon green ball in stride. It took off at a sharp angle away from us but banged off the curb and ricocheted back across his path and into mine. I blocked it with my outside foot, and it rolled slowly ahead of us and into the gutter.

"I mean, you have to notice how self-conscious I get when your friends are talking about watches that cost more than my tour van."

Howard veered a few steps off course to retrieve the ball with his toe. He scooted it ahead of me, and it paused at the crest of the road.

"Or like," I continued, "when everyone was interested in the website I use for cheap airfare, but when they realized I was flying coach, they just stopped paying attention to me. It was embarrassing."

I kicked the ball a little harder than I intended, and it bounced ahead several yards into a cul-de-sac.

"It was like they discovered that I don't belong in this group."

We walked in silence for a minute until we stopped in the wide-open area at the end of the road. Away from the hedgerows, we could see much more of the sky. I kicked the ball back to Howard, who had already turned around. I wondered what he was thinking.

"Anyway," I continued, "it's not fair to you, and I apologize. I just need to be better about interacting with your wealthy friends. And I really need to stop feeling like I'm less than someone with more money."

Howard nudged the ball ahead, back the way we came. It had been a while since he had spoken.

"You could've made six figures as a CPA, Mike," he said, tapping the ball a second time. "You chose to follow your passion instead."

The ball rolled to me, and I gave it a soft kick. It occurred to me that not a single car or person had passed us on our walk. We had the whole street to ourselves.

"I can't even tell you how much I respect you for that."

We were quiet again for several paces. The bright August sun was heating up the morning. My tank top started to show sweat.

"Thanks," I finally said.

We kicked the ball back and forth until we were nearly back, discussing our plans for the rest of the week. One of us eventually bounced the ball through a gate. We kept walking.

"Babe," Howard said, stopping as we approached the house. "I'm proud of you."

I stopped too.

"You work hard," he continued. "And your passion is sexy."

I took his hand and shuffled to match his stride—left and left, right and right—as we walked up the driveway in step.

He squeezed. "I'm grateful for the miracle that allowed us to find each other."

"Me too," I said.

Via Chicago

14

Nashville was becoming a place where only my stuff lived, and I wondered if I was missing out.

Just before the pandemic, I showed up in Music City with no industry connections, so I lugged my keyboard to writer's rounds every night, trying to make myself known. By the second month I was named a "Local Artist of the Week" by Lightning 100FM, an influential radio station. It felt like I'd found my place. But it turns out, there are a lot of talented musicians and songwriters with the same plan.

The phrase "Ten Year Town" came up in dozens of conversations while waiting my turn to get on stage. From fellow newbies to grizzled veterans, everyone agreed on one thing—no one succeeds in Nashville without paying dues.

I wondered if over a decade of Chicago dues transferred, like college credits.

The answer came, appropriately, in song form. An older gentleman took the stage at a writer's round and introduced himself as a "unicorn," which is what native Nashvillians are often called. In his song, "Ten Year Town," he mocked songwriters who come to Nashville to make it big, only to move back home after a year. I sipped my whiskey indignantly.

That's not going to be me, I vowed.

Two years later, I felt torn. A pandemic, pericarditis, a broken engagement, and an incredible new man in my life had changed my perspective on paying dues. Waiting around to play one song at writer's rounds seemed like a waste of time now. Life with Howard felt important, exciting, and I didn't want to miss a minute of it.

I had to find a better way into the Nashville scene, but there was no time to figure it out now. I returned from the Hamptons, and the next day drove up to Chicago for some gigs.

The City of Big Shoulders will always feel like home. I lived there for twelve years—countless shows, late-night hangs, and jam sessions with my musician friends were formative moments in my adult life. And I came out during that time, so my authentic self was born there.

I was back in town to play keys on Nathan Graham's new album, *Saint of Second Chances*. A gifted and soulful singer and guitarist, years ago he was tempted to give up playing music. That was around when I began to suspect that my own band had peaked and considered going solo.

We met playing a Bob Dylan tribute night at a DIY venue called the Red Room, loved each other's sets, and over several rounds of beers decided that we needed to work together. I produced his next collection of songs, and he played guitar on my first solo album in a decade. We spent a lot of time together in the studio and forged a bond, helping spark the next phase of each other's careers.

We took a break from the studio session, catching up on current events in our lives. I bragged about my incredible new man. And then I opened up about a concern that I'd not yet voiced aloud.

I worried that I was simply filling a role, as Howard's first crush was also a Catholic Scorpio football captain from Ohio. What if he suddenly got over his infatuation with me? Howard would just continue living his life.

"But," I said, "I can't get used to living in a nice place, flying first class, and staying in fancy hotels, because for me it'd be a long way down back to life before Howard."

"Would you say it'd be a long, long, long... long way down?" Nathan quoted one of my songs at me. I laughed.

"You know what I mean."

"Man," he said, "first of all, it wouldn't be that long of a fall. You're doing fine, and you don't like all that fancy shit, anyway."

"Sure."

"And second of all, it sounds like this guy is dope, and it sounds like he really loves you."

I nodded.

"And it sounds like you really love him, too."

"Yeah, like a lot."

"So just go with it. If it doesn't work out, you've got options. Stay in Nashville, or move back to Chicago. There's always a place for you here, man."

Sometimes you really need to hear your best friends say what you're suspecting for it to crystallize. Nathan had to remind me that I liked my life. I wasn't living the "A" dream of traveling the world with my best friends from my college band. I was living the "B" dream of being a mostly full-time musician, gigging and touring while maintaining a flexible side job. And really, my job was pretty good, because it was my own web design business. I was the boss. I could give myself time off to be creative whenever I needed to.

And I could do it from anywhere.

Our House

15

Two days after returning from Chicago, I was back on a plane from Nashville to L.A. It was now August. Howard was having knee surgery, and I insisted on coming to look after him.

I had homework to do on the flight; Howard had forwarded the hospital's surgical instructions. I went over the pre-op orders with him in advance:

> Did you see this part?
> No smoking a week before surgery. Does that include weed?

> Standard Gremlins rules apply the night before. No eating or drinking after midnight.

> Also probably don't get you wet or you'll multiply

> And I got the post-op stuff. I'll be your murse

Nurse Mike. Hot.

When I arrived, Howard's building felt less intimidating. The courtyard with its towering trees and tropical plants felt more inviting and less like *Jurassic Park*. Or at least I felt more like Jeff Goldblum, certain of my place in the franchise, and less like Newman. We all knew Newman was gonna get it.

This time when Howard opened the door, Nacho jumped up on me right away.

"You're in," Howard said, smiling. "That means he likes you."

"I like youuu," I said melodically.

"Aw babe," Howard said as he wrapped me in his arms, squeezing Nacho between us. "I'm growing quite fond of you."

We kissed. Nacho let me go and hopped around, barking, and Curtis waddled over to investigate my bag.

"I wanna show you something," Howard said. He grabbed my suitcase and started up the stairs. Peeking into his office, I noticed that he had replaced my "Play Like a Champion Today" selfie with a different photo of me.

I followed him into his bedroom closet. Straight ahead were white floor-to-ceiling drawers and cabinets, to the left were hanging rods, with shirts and slacks all perfectly in place.

To the right were floor-to-ceiling shelves. He gestured to an empty space.

"That's yours, sweetheart," he said.

"You cleared off a shelf for me?!"

"Yeah. And this, too."

He went to the back of the room and opened a drawer. It was completely empty, except for a yellow tin harmonica case.

"That's for you," he said. "Not sure where it came from, figured you'd be able to use it. You're like Stevie, you can play anything."

"Not like Stevie does, though." I put my backpack down and picked up the box. It was old and starting to rust. I pulled out the harmonica and blew into it a few times. The notes came out muddy and lacked any distinguishable melody.

"No idea how he does what he does on this thing," I chuckled.

I could tell Howard was excited about taking this step. But he was justifiably guarded. Howard's home was finely tuned, like living in a Stradivarius violin. Every square inch was carefully considered as a part of the whole. Except now a string had been taken off, left for me to replace. This level of vulnerability was clearly not typical for Howard Bragman. I finally got the picture. This was not just an infatuation. This is what true love looked like for him.

"You gave me a place in your space!" I said as I hugged him.

"You can thank me by filling my space," he said mischievously. "After tomorrow morning, it's going to be a while before we can fool around again."

On the drive to the hospital, Howard told me that walking down the street kicking a ball was the best part of our Hamptons trip. Not the fancy dinner we had at an exclusive country club, not boating with his friends, not dining with celebrities, and not even the sexy young men in the pool. The highlight for him was kicking a ball back and forth while we shared what was in our hearts. I agreed.

I contemplated this while waiting in a nearby coffee shop during his surgery. If that was all we needed, we were destined for a lifetime of happiness together.

Something told me I should move in with Howard. However long "a lifetime" turned out to be, I wanted all of it with him.

My lease back in Nashville was up in six weeks. But I knew that I had more to accomplish in Music City. I had an auspicious start there, but the pandemic lockdown put an end to that, and then getting pericarditis delayed my comeback. I was torn. Move in with the love of my life in L.A., or give it more time in Nashville?

The morning after his surgery, I slipped out of bed before Howard woke up.

I returned to the bedroom as he started to stir.

"Good morning I love you," I said, presenting him with one of his baby blue coffee mugs.

"Good morning lover," he said groggily, scratching his chest. He yawned and stretched. It made me think of Baloo from *The Jungle Book*. I stood next to him.

"How's your leg?"

"Actually, not too bad," he said. "I don't think I need the painkillers." He accepted his coffee.

"They told me I can walk on it right away, so you're off the hook, murse Mike."

"So I didn't have to wake up at the ass-crack of dawn to get you a coffee?"

"Afraid not babe." He took a sip.

"Too bad," I said. "I was looking forward to pampering you."

"Well, nobody has ever brought me coffee in bed before."

"Shut up."

"Yeah," he said, with trace amounts of disdain.

"Weren't you married for like, twelve years?"

"Sixteen," he said.

"And haven't you had like a half dozen guys stay with you since then?"

"Yes, dear."

"Oh my God, Howard. I'm sorry." My heart sank for him. Howard made his livelihood by meeting the needs of everyone else, and he'd never had a partner do something as simple as bring him coffee in bed.

"It's okay," he said. "I've got you now."

"I'm giving you a rain check on this murse situation," I said. "This was too easy."

Looking back, I regret voicing that thought aloud. But no one could have anticipated the diagnosis Howard would face in just over five months. I'd tend to him then—bathe him, hold his hand through the pain, and while he rested, temper my own fears long enough to update his worried friends and family.

For now, I simply propped up his leg with a pillow, put his ice pack in place, and got back in bed next to him.

"Babe," he said. "When you're a big famous music star, are you going to want a teammate instead of a coach?"

I laughed.

"Seriously."

"Howard," I started.

He cut me off. "It's okay if you do. Just make sure he likes older men, too, so we can have a throuple."

"This just sounds like something you've been fantasizing about."

"I can't imagine my life without you. That first weekend, I told you, I felt it. There was electricity. I didn't want to scare you off. But I knew it already. I want to spend the rest of my life with you."

"Me too," I said.

"You want to spend the rest of your life with yourself?!" he said.

I never stopped falling for that trap.

"You just want me because I check the boxes of your first love," I tested.

"You're available. He wasn't."

That wasn't quite the right way to say it, but I knew what he meant. I had quiet crushes on straight men, too. It's part of the silent torture that gay men endure.

"Should we move in together?" I asked after a moment. He didn't answer right away. He knew exactly why I was hesitant—my career. We weren't concerned about the fact that we had known each other for just under six months.

"How about this. When my leg heals, I'll come to Nashville. I have clients there and I can find more work. I'll take some meetings. Let me see your place. We can split our time between there and here."

When Howard was back on his feet a few days later, I returned to Nashville. Back in my little apartment I lugged my laundry downstairs, across the parking lot, and down another flight of stairs into the laundry room. Three of the washers were broken (one sat filled with disgusting brown water), and two of the dryers were known to steal quarters.

I suddenly felt self-conscious. This didn't seem like a place Howard would live.

Head Over Feet

16

September 26, 2022. Nashville, Tennessee. Seven months since our first chat on Scruff.

I woke up in my own bed expecting to see Howard next to me. He was visiting my apartment for the first time.

But my bed was empty—no Howard, and my two extra pillows were gone. The opposite side of the comforter was pulled back, indicating his exit at some point during the night.

My modest one-bedroom apartment suited me fine. But maybe it had scared Howard off already. Nothing hung on my plain white bedroom walls. I had trouble turning off my brain at the end of the day, and I'd read somewhere that an empty bedroom helped to clear the mind for recharging overnight.

Shuffling into my living room, I was relieved to see Howard sitting on my couch. He had found a blanket in my closet, which was now folded on one side of him, with two king-size pillows stacked on the other. He wore nothing but reading glasses and orange boxer briefs, and was tapping away on his tablet's attached keyboard, which he had set on a TV tray in front of him. He had already made coffee which he drank from one of my "Mike Maimone" branded mugs.

I paused in the entryway to let reality sink in. For seven months I sat here, falling deeper in love with the voice on the other end of the phone. And now, that voice and the beautiful man who generated it were here, in my little world.

He looked delightfully out of place. My distinguished older boyfriend was no longer in his office with his curated furniture and art collection. He now sat on my turquoise couch between my mismatched thrift store end tables and lamps, surrounded by my brightly colored acoustic treatments. Covering the floor was a fluffy purple rug. My vibrant colorful studio was also my living and dining area. Even Willy Wonka might balk at throwing a dinner party here.

Howard looked up.

"Did I snore?" I asked.

"No, babe," Howard said through a yawn. "I just find the couch more comfortable sometimes."

"Liar," I said, crossing the room and sitting next to him. He was wrapping up an email. I leaned over and kissed him on his temple.

"Good morning I love you," I whispered, putting an arm around him. "I can't believe you're really here."

"Good morning, sweet angel," he said, leaning into me. He hit send on the email, took off his glasses, and turned to kiss me. "How did you sleep?"

"Like a brick," I replied. "You? Were you alright on the couch?"

"I slept great. But you're going to have to get rid of this carpet when we get a place together. I almost tripped on it when I got up to pee."

I winced at the idea of Howard falling on his first night in my home. But I also wasn't about to give it up.

"Sure, we can put it in whatever room I turn into the studio, then you won't have to walk on it much."

"And we're not putting the studio in the living room, right, mister?" Howard smiled and pulled me in close.

"Right."

In the time between my last L.A. trip and Howard's Nashville visit, we set in motion a plan to live together. We agreed that it was too soon for me to move to California. I had just played the main stage of Nashville Pride, and it felt like things were back on track for me in Music City. I couldn't pack up and leave town now.

The solution was for Howard to find work in Nashville, and we would rent a house together. We would split our time between the two. His only caveat was that I couldn't take over the living room with my recording studio, and that seemed reasonable to me.

We each had one of the non-dairy protein shakes I'd bought for Howard. He'd sent me a grocery list: unsweetened lemonade and iced tea, cheddar Smart Pop, fresh fruit, almond milk, Kashi with protein, smooches, hugs, and a couple of other things I can't mention. Then we headed down to my vehicle—a 15-passenger tour van.

"It puts the lotion in the basket," Howard drawled as he climbed up and into my ride for the first time. There were a few dents and the windows were blacked out to hide our gear.

"What? Oh," I said. "Yeah, we definitely need to find a rental where we can dig a pit in the basement."

"We've already got the creeper van," he concurred.

On day one of our house search, we were guided by a friend of one of Howard's real estate agent contacts. He had lined up five places to look at, each more modern and expensive than the last. My rent was around $1,200 a month, and we were looking for something less than double that. The agent's final selection was a brand-new three-story townhouse renting for over $5,000 a month. We asked the agent if he had anything in the $2,000 range. His face went blank. It appeared our request did not compute, and we went our separate ways.

As we drove back to my apartment I said, "I don't think that guy understood our objectives."

"I think his friend told him that I was looking for a place and he assumed it was for me, babe."

"Yeah," I said. "You're so accomplished."

"Aw babe, my greatest accomplishment is having you by my side."

I melted a little, then wondered if I liked being thought of as an "accomplishment," then decided not to nitpick.

"Okay, so I found some places on Craigslist that are less fancy to look at tomorrow."

We returned to my apartment, where I made dinner for Howard. It was my usual—chicken breast and sweet potatoes in the air fryer, microwaved veggies, and a big salad. Howard stood in the kitchen doorway as I worked. He had changed into shorts and a tank top, and I was in my usual outfit.

"I love that you're a nudist," Howard giggled. "But don't hurt yourself."

"I'll be careful," I said, cubing the sweet potatoes. I seasoned them with Jamaican spice and transferred them to the air fryer. "Ten minutes to go, can you grab your drink and set up the TV trays please?"

Howard concocted his Arnold Palmer and went to the other room. When I brought dinner out, he was waiting patiently on the couch. I set down both plates, two small bowls of salad, and placed steak knives and forks on top of paper towels.

"What, no napkins?" Howard scoffed playfully, rolling his eyes.

"I mean, paper towels do the same thing," I said as I sat next to him. "I don't buy Kleenex, either. Toilet paper works."

"You're such a bro," Howard said, taking a bite of sweet potato.

"But these are fantastic," he said. "My bro can cook!"

We watched an episode of *The White Lotus* on my laptop. I had been a little nervous that Howard would be uncomfortable in my small apartment, but he seemed content. And I couldn't have been happier about that.

I knew that my place was unconventional. A desk with studio monitors took the place of a dining room table. But it worked for me. After six- and seven-year relationships back-to-back, I needed a pause on domestic life. I just wanted a place to create.

On the other hand, the homes Howard had owned were beautiful and even featured in glossy design magazines. He had a way of making light of our differences without making me the butt of the joke. He poked fun at himself for liking fancy things as he observed how little use I had for them. He told me often how he respected me, my thriftiness, and my hard work. He always made sure that part was clear.

The next day, we found a two-bedroom house in Inglewood that was within our budget and available immediately. He'd take the second bedroom for his Nashville office, and I had an attic area for my studio (where he could avoid my purple rug). We signed the lease on the spot.

During our first seven months together, I often worried that Howard and I were too far apart in age, physical distance, income tax bracket, and pace of life. There was a cultural chasm between us. Our social circles were very different. I accused him of being merely infatuated with me—a space-filler for his first man crush. I put up walls to protect myself from the inevitability of him moving on once he tired of our fling.

Now Howard was moving to Nashville for me.

Summertime

After signing our first lease together, we went to Atlanta so I could meet Howard's brother, Alan, and two nephews.

I had heard a lot about Adam and David; they were very special to Howard. I was a little nervous about how they would receive me, being just a few years older than them.

Soon after meeting, they eased my trepidation by informing me that compared to Howard's recent boyfriends, I was "age appropriate."

We talked sports—they knew as much about my Cleveland Browns as I did—and they shared stories about visiting Uncle Howard in Hollywood and meeting all kinds of celebrities when they were younger.

When we left, they told me that they hadn't seen their uncle so happy in years. It was clear how much they meant to each other. Thankfully, Atlanta and Nashville are close so we would be together often.

On our last day back in Music City, Howard threw a barbecue at Olivia Hill's house.

Apparently, this was a habit of his; wherever he was in the country, Howard could bring catering and a few dozen friends to someone's house and have a party. We filled the back of my van with trays from Martin's Bar-B-Que Joint and headed over to the West Side.

Most of the attendees were guests of Howard's and Olivia's. I was glad that two of my closest friends were able to make it so I could introduce Howard to my drummer, Rob Gould, and fellow singer/songwriter Phillip-Michael Scales.

Phillip-Michael and I met in Chicago sometime in the early 2010s. It's impossible to pinpoint our first meeting—we were always on tour, running into each other at festivals and shows. We had the same booking agent at the time and the same determination to make music for a living. He moved to Nashville a few months before I did, and we both hit the ground running. We'd often meet for coffee and compare notes on everything from songwriting and mental health to hiring band members and navigating our love lives. I was there for him through a breakup with a girlfriend, and he was there for me when my fiancé and I called it quits.

We were close but didn't get into details. So it may have caught Phillip-Michael off guard when Howard told him, "Just look at my man! No need for boner pills with this one."

Who says that? To a straight guy? Within a couple hours of meeting? Howard did. Regardless of who he was with, he was unfiltered—and miraculously, it came off as charming.

Dinner and drinks were winding down, and about a dozen of us sat on Olivia's back porch talking. I reclined at one end of a sofa, and Howard leaned against me as we all chatted. It felt surprisingly normal. Our friends didn't care that we were twenty-five years apart in age; they were just happy we were happy. My insecurities about our differences were melting away.

I thanked Olivia for hosting and for being the reason Howard and I were together.

When we first chatted earlier that year, on his birthday, Howard had been on Scruff scouting men in Nashville because he thought he'd be visiting for work.

Olivia is a trans woman and Navy combat veteran who had been treated abusively while working at the Vanderbilt University power plant. She sued for workplace discrimination, and her attorney contacted Howard to help publicize the situation. Howard signed on pro bono but never had to visit Nashville. Vanderbilt settled with Olivia out of court.

She went on to become the first trans person elected to public office in Tennessee.

Right from the start, before his success and notoriety, before he had any leverage in the entertainment world, Howard was an advocate for LGBTQ+ rights. Amplifying unheard voices in his community was a mission Howard carried in his heart and soul. I didn't know it at the time, but Olivia Hill was the most recent of countless individuals he'd helped, and she wouldn't be the last.

My Baby Loves Me

18

Howard flew back to Los Angeles. Two weeks later we were supposed to meet in Chicago—I was proudly providing a weeklong romantic getaway during peak autumn color in western Michigan.

The plan had been for Howard to spend the weekend in Chicago while I made some money at back-to-back wedding gigs in Nashville. Then I'd fly in on Sunday, rent a car, pick him up, and drive us to a cabin I'd rented near Saugatuck.

I've learned that man makes plans and God laughs.

The previous week, Howard's Aunt Barbara had fallen and broken her hip. At age eighty-five, the whole family was concerned. For a couple of days, she appeared to be healing. But mid-week, she developed a blood clot and passed away.

Howard took his planned flight to Chicago, but instead of spending the weekend catching up with friends, he got a ride to the funeral in Flint from his Aunt Manya, Barbara's sister. The new plan was for him to take the Amtrak on Monday morning, and I'd pick him up in Kalamazoo.

On Sunday evening I landed in Chicago and checked in.

> **Landed. Love you so much. How are you holding up?**

> We cried.
> Now we eat.

As I waited in line for my rental car, I thought about the two of us in Michigan, but with Howard alone at a hotel, and me alone in a cabin. It didn't make any sense to me. Then I pictured Howard riding the train by himself and called an audible.

> **What hotel are you in? I want to come there tonight**

> It's in Flint

> **I know. What hotel?** 🖤
> **Google says I'll be in Flint by 10:30**

Howard sent me the hotel information. Twenty-three minutes later he texted:

> My baby loves me 🖤

Flint is about five hours from O'Hare, a little over two hours past Saugatuck. I'd done longer drives overnight on tour. It wasn't a question that I would go out of my way to get him.

It was after midnight by the time I parked the rental car outside the hotel. Howard had added me to the reservation so I could get a key and slip into the room without disturbing his sleep.

As I hit the elevator button, I compared this hotel room meeting to our previous one—the first time we met.

My life had completely changed in just five months. Ascending in the elevator at the Royalton in New York City, I was excited, nervous, and horny. I was about to finally meet my phone pal in person.

This time, the feelings were much more potent. The connection was much deeper. Unbelievably so, given how little time had passed.

Responsibility. Compassion. Ownership. He was mine. Not a possession—a companion to care for.

I slid the key card quietly into the lock, trying to enter the room stealthily. My grieving boyfriend had an emotional day and needed his sleep. The door closed behind me.

"My baby loves me," I heard him murmur through pitch blackness.

Flint City Shake It

19

The next morning, we went on an "origins of Howard" tour. I was excited to see where he came from. He tempered my expectations.

"Flint ain't the same place it was when I grew up."

"That's okay, I want to see."

We drove by the houses he and his family lived in, his schools, and his synagogue, a midcentury modern structure that had been converted to a Baptist church. Some areas looked nice. Manicured lawns and shiny cars in the driveways. Suburban.

But at one point Howard had me pull over so he could get out to take a picture. I looked across the street and through the house to my left. There had been a fire some time ago, but nobody bothered to tear down the charred shell of a building that remained. Next door was a vacant lot, with trash scattered across gravel and waist-high weeds. On the other side was a house whose front porch had collapsed, so it was either vacant or the residents used another entrance.

I didn't see anyone out and about. Which unfortunately made sense. What was there to walk to? There were no open stores or businesses, and most of the houses seemed empty. It was difficult to picture anyone existing, let alone thriving in this neighborhood.

But as we drove, Howard recounted stories about his family, friends, and local businesses, and slowly I started to see Flint through his eyes. When Howard was a kid, Flint was the second largest city in Michigan behind Detroit. It was a center of prosperity during the golden age of the automobile industry. It was a community where people of different faiths and ethnicities prospered together.

True, Flint had seen better days. But it was still full of resilient people doing their best to make lives for their families.

Everything clicked. Flint is where Howard Bragman learned his superpowers: his empathy, his authenticity, his ambition, his ability to relate to all sorts of people, and his appreciation for anyone trying to carve out their own place in the world.

Gimme Some

20

We made it across the state to Saugatuck just after nightfall. The sky opened, and the windshield wipers couldn't keep up with the downpour. We got off the freeway several miles south of town. At the top of the ramp there were no streetlights. I took a right, the headlamps revealing dense woods to either side of us. A few hundred yards down, the road came to a T. There was no street sign, but I knew my way. Another right. Lake Michigan was a dark void to our left. The only visible landmarks were the nearest tree trunks to our right, with branches reaching eerily above us as we passed.

"Where are you taking me, babe?" Howard teased. He sounded tired, but up for adventure.

"If I was going to abduct you, don't you think I would've already done it in my creeper van?" I countered.

"Can't abduct the willing," he said.

A few minutes later we slowed, took a right, and pulled into the gravel drive of Timber Bluff. My friends Mike and Jeff own it, and for the past ten years, I managed their website in exchange for an off-season stay. I hadn't been able to take them up on it since moving to Nashville in 2020, so I was excited to return. It was a special place to me and I wanted to share it with Howard.

But I was also a bit apprehensive. This place wasn't as fancy as the hotels we stayed in when Howard booked the accommodations.

We rolled past the first few cabins.

Also weighing on me was the memory of bringing my ex-fiancé to stay in one of these cabins several years ago. He complained about everything, and we left early. I shook my head and tried to block out that memory as we pulled into our parking spot. Suddenly, I felt stressed out about my decision to bring us there.

"We don't have an umbrella, do we?" I asked.

"Of course we do," Howard said, producing an extendable travel umbrella.

"Wow, you really do think of everything," I said, impressed. "Be prepared—like the Boy Scouts' motto."

"I'll be your scoutmaster," he joked creepily. "Or you can be mine." He opened the door, filling the car abruptly with the noise of heavy rainfall.

I hustled from the driver's side to the front porch while Howard circumnavigated the car under his umbrella. A tiny overhang shielded us at the entrance, but the wind off the lake blew the rain at us sideways. The door was locked. A number pad lit up, reminding me that I had been given a code when I booked our reservation.

I could see Howard in my peripheral vision, just over my shoulder, steadying the umbrella against the gusts with both hands. I fumbled with my phone to find the numbers we needed for entrance.

In my mind, I felt my ex's impatient glare burning a hole through me, accompanied by "Come onnnnn!" and "How did you not think of this before you got out of the car?!" It had been sixteen months since we'd broken up, but Butch still lived rent-free in my head, making me anxious in situations like this.

I found the code, punched it in, and opened the door. I turned to look at Howard. He was perfectly content. Wet, but content.

We took in the interior. The kitchen opened into the living area, with wooden walls and beams on the pitched ceiling, a fluffy brown couch on one end and a stone fireplace on the other.

"Cozy," Howard said. "Nice job, babe. I love it."

My self-imposed anxiety vanished, replaced first by embarrassment for again comparing Howard with my ex, then by appreciation for the effortless ways in which Howard soothed me.

We unloaded the car together. Howard held the umbrella while I lugged our bags and groceries. He'd also brought a bag of leftovers from his aunt's shiva. We put the food in the fridge. I wanted to go right to sleep, but Howard always unpacked the moment he arrived, so I joined him. Then we finally called it a night.

"Good night, my sweet angel," Howard said as we held each other. "Thank you for coming all the way to get me. My man is such a mensch."

I had forgotten about that part, focusing instead on my perceived deficiencies. We tend to be our own harshest critics. Howard didn't see anything wrong today. He was helping me pave over my traumatic memories, replacing a bumpy road with a smooth future. Being with Howard brought me closer to the best version of myself.

When I awoke the next morning, Howard was already up. The rain had stopped. After a cup of coffee and an email check, we headed out to meet one of his friends. Although I had booked this week, anywhere we went, Howard had people to see.

On the drive into town, we passed two infamous Saugatuck haunts: Campit and The Dunes. The former is a gay campground, known as a popular cruising spot. The latter is a gay resort known for its dance club and pool parties. I told Howard that I'd never gone to either.

"I've never stayed at Campit, babe, but I've definitely been there!" Howard cackled.

"We have very different Saugatucks," I said with a smile.

"Yeah," he said mischievously, "mine is the fun one."

Back at the cabin that evening, Howard went to the bathroom, and I turned on the gas fire and put the couch cushions on the floor in front of the fireplace. I sat on one and waited for him to come back into the room. I patted a cushion, inviting Howard to join me. He obliged. I pulled him close to me and kissed him.

"I've always wanted to make love by a fire," I said, laying him back. We kissed for a while. The cushions slid apart, leaving him squished between me and the hard floor.

"It's a little uncomfortable, my lummox," Howard said.

"Yeah, this did not go as planned," I said with dismay.

We stood up and moved to the bed, undressing along the way.

After making love in a more comfortable setting, we hopped in the shower together. We talked about everything and nothing while we washed and rinsed one another. College football. Moving in together. My new songs. We turned off the shower and got out. As we dried off, Howard noticed that I was a little… excited.

"You ready again?!" he exclaimed.

"I mean yeah, look at you!" I said grinning, hanging my towel on a hook.

"My man is a machine," he giggled.

"You're just…" I sighed. "You're literally everything I've always wanted."

My ex-fiancé had convinced me that I had a problem, that being attracted to older men was a mental illness. It got to me, and I sought help. I went to three different therapists, hoping to pray the gray away. But they all told me the same thing: people are attracted to who they're attracted to. If it's two consenting adults, don't worry about what that looks like.

Thanks to therapy, I started to believe that I wasn't broken after all. I pictured the man of my dreams. He had kind eyes and was generous with his smile. He had salt-and-pepper hair, and he was tall and beefy—perfect for cuddling—with a burly chest.

I just described Howard's physical appearance. And here he was in front of me, naked, skin glistening, damp chest hair. I was at full salute.

"Here babe, hold this." He handed me his towel, without putting it in my hands. It hung between my legs.

"You're such a stud. Keep it there." He picked up his phone. I flashed a goofy smile, and he snapped a picture.

"Mind if I send this to a friend?"

"Why?" I asked.

"I want to show off my hot trick."

I groaned and walked into the kitchen.

"Aw babe, come on, here, the lighting is better in the living room."

He snapped another picture and sat down on the couch to text it.

"Seriously," I said. "Who are you sending that to?"

"I just want to show you off to a couple of my friends," he said. "They're sweet, you'll love them. They're intergenerational, too."

"You want us to fool around with them," I said.

"Someday. You'll like the older one."

We needed a snack. I pulled out the bag he had brought from his aunt's shiva.

"And how are you feeling, honey?" I asked.

"I'm sad, sweetheart. But thanks for asking." He told me about his Aunt Barb, and I listened while I prepared tuna salad bagels.

I opened another container full of what looked like baked pasta. It was cut into cubes. I took a tiny bite of one. My eyes shot open as wide as dinner plates. Howard burst into laughter.

"What *is* this?!" I asked. I shoved the rest of the piece in my mouth and grabbed two more.

"It's called kugel, sweetness," he laughed. "I make a really good one."

No Time at All

21

Howard and I walked down the middle of the street on a bluff overlooking Lake Michigan. Not a cloud in the sky on our last morning stroll in Saugatuck. Vibrant autumn leaves glowed in the sunshine, clinging to their branches despite a brisk breeze.

I often made Howard stand still so I could photograph him. He always dressed sharply, and this was my first chance to see his cold-weather looks. I stopped to admire him, but he kept walking, looking at his phone. In the golden morning light, he appeared painted into a backdrop of red, yellow, and orange leaves.

"Hold it," I said. I framed him in my camera app. He stopped and turned to me, still looking down.

"Yes, dear," he said, distracted.

"Come on," I implored. "You look amazing right now."

He looked up, eyebrows raised, head tilted to the side.

"You're a faaaag," he teased, fluffing the "f" playfully and singing the rest of the abrasive slur. This was his way of saying, "You're in love with me and I know it."

"Hey!" I snapped. "You can't call me that!"

"Would homo be better?"

"Come on, mister, let me get a good one of you."

He relented and flashed his brilliant smile.

"You're gorgeous," I said.

He removed his sunglasses, spread his arms out, and I snapped a photo. A couple days later, he posted it on his Instagram. The caption read:

> It's not my official birthday, but nonetheless an auspicious day—I'm 2/3 of 100 years old today. I am grateful for my health, my family, my friends, my business colleagues and clients and "my man" who stirs my heart and soul.
> As Irene Ryan sang in Pippin, "Now, I've known the fears of sixty-six years / I've had troubles and tears by the score / But the only thing I'd trade them for / Is sixty-seven more…"
> It's time to start living. With so much gratitude.
>

It was October 24, 2022, eight months after Howard's sixty-sixth birthday. I had planned a party for him in Chicago to celebrate his 66.667 remarkable years on the planet.

That morning, I had a recording session at Shirk Studios. A few weeks earlier, a TikTok I posted from a recent Nashville gig had gotten 50,000 views overnight. It was my cover of "Before He Cheats" by Carrie Underwood, in which I change the lyric from "right now, he's probably slow dancing with a bleach-blonde tramp who's trying to get frisky" to "bleach-blonde twink." I thought this could be my viral moment. Friends of mine in a band called Durry had one a few months earlier. Now they were selling out clubs across the country. But Howard, as usual, cautioned me lovingly.

"It's a great cover," he said. "You should definitely record it. I just don't want you to be hurt if this isn't the moment your career takes off."

I thanked him for his concern, but reminded him that I'd been doing this for almost twenty years. There had been dozens of these moments that never materialized.

"Don't worry, I'm never actually excited until the money is in the bank," I told him.

There was nothing I'd rather do than make music. No matter how many times my hopes soared and crashed, I always dusted myself off and got up again.

I've had several short flights. Playing on late night TV, performing at Lollapalooza, headlining the legendary Metro in Chicago, touring with some of my favorite bands, and landing songs in TV shows. Getting 10,000 new TikTok followers overnight felt like we were buckled up, tray tables stowed, ready to blast down the runway again. I called my Chicago band, and we arranged my subversive version of the country hit.

As we recorded, I kept an eye on the clock. I was not going to be late for the dinner party I had arranged.

Even the best laid plans.

We called a wrap on the tracking, dumped the files on a hard drive, and I changed clothes in the studio bathroom. By the time I hopped in a car, the party was getting underway. I texted my ETA to Howard, about fifteen minutes late.

When I finally arrived at Mia Francesca's in Wrigleyville, I peeked in the front window. I could see the group toward the back of the restaurant. I slipped in the front door, introduced myself to the host, and handed him four large plastic cake-topper numbers—three sixes and one seven—plus a candle.

He looked at me like I'd just handed him a wet kitten.

"What would you like me to do with these?"

I flashed him my cutest grin. This man was the linchpin in my surprise, one that I had planned several weeks in advance. I needed to win him over.

"See that gorgeous gentleman over there?"

He turned with the enthusiasm of a barbecue pitmaster hired to cater a vegan wedding.

"That's my husband. Today we're celebrating the fact that he's been alive for two-thirds of a century."

"Clever," said our host. "He's sixty-six point six-seven. Got it." His frown relaxed. I counted this as a victory and headed toward the table.

Howard was glowing, surrounded by his friends and family. He wore a cashmere sweater, his hair neatly combed, and his goatee trimmed tight. His broad smile seemed permanently affixed to his face as he spoke.

"There he is! My man threw me a party!" he said as I approached. I apologized to the table for being late. Howard's Aunt Manya sat at one end, my friends Eshanthika and Zac at the other. In between were seven of Howard's friends, three of whom I'd met the previous June. The space to Howard's right was empty, left open for me.

I greeted everyone and thanked them for coming before claiming my spot.

After we smooched hello and he asked me about my recording session, Howard put a hand on my thigh and leaned over, his nose gently nuzzling my ear.

"Just do me a favor," he whispered. "No singing."

"You got it," I whispered back, squeezing his knee.

Uh oh, I thought. When someone brings a cake with lit candles, you can't keep people from singing "Happy Birthday."

I handed Howard a card. "Here you go, honey," I said.

He opened the green envelope. Inside was a one-hundredth birthday card, only I had cut a third off of the bottom. The inside read, "Happy 100th Birthday!" I had squeezed in a tiny "2/3 of" just before the 1.

He laughed out loud and passed the card to his friends. "Cute. Thanks, babe." He put his arm around me, pulled me close, and kissed my cheek. "And we're going to have forty more years together."

"I'm planning on it," I said. "At least forty more."

Dinner was a joyous occasion, and our respective friends got along fabulously. My insecurities about our differences were long gone.

Each time I met another planet in Howard's orbit, I learned more about what a magnanimous center of gravity he was. He helped so many people to jumpstart their careers, or find love, or fix some crisis situation. I'd known him just eight months, already considered him my closest friend, but suspected that I was still only scratching the surface of who Howard Bragman was. It was thrilling.

After many bottles of wine had been emptied and our stomachs were full, our host emerged from the kitchen. He carried a dinner plate with an enormous serving of tiramisu. He was finally smiling, candlelight illuminating his face. The lit numbers hung on for dear life, crowding onto the dessert. I tried to make the signal for "no singing," but it was no use.

"Haaaaappy birthday to youuuu," sang the table. Howard took it all in, smiling with his whole face. I joined the choir.

"Happy birthday to you!
Happy birthday dear Howwwww-arrrrrrrrd!
Happy birthday to you!"

Howard beamed at his friends, then blew out the candles.

When the party was over, we found ourselves back at the hotel. I had put on our favorite Rat Pack playlist and we were getting ready for bed.

"Hey Mike?" Howard said.

"Yes, Howard?" I said, mirroring his formal tone.

"I love you so much."

I stood behind him, looking at us both in the mirror over his shoulder. My left hand wrapped around his waist, pulling his back into my chest, and I held a toothbrush in my right hand.

"I love you, too," I said. We swayed to the soothing sound of Sammy Davis Jr.'s voice as we brushed our teeth together.

Right One

Pericarditis was so debilitating that I thought I'd never sing my songs again. But it also slowed me down, allowing me to fall in love with Howard.

Back in September 2021, however—five months before I encountered my soulmate on Scruff—I couldn't fathom it being a *good* thing that it felt like my collarbones were being pried off.

The pain was excruciating—and terrifying. My ex-fiancé and I had finally parted ways, so I was alone in my new apartment.

When the paramedics arrived, I explained through gasps for air that I had recurrent pericarditis. The heart usually functions normally during a flare, and once they determined that my life wasn't in jeopardy, they left me waiting in the emergency department for hours. No matter how much I insisted, they wouldn't give me anything for the pain. I wished I could pass out.

My parents had to drive to Nashville from North Carolina to tend to me in my apartment. The pain was so intense for another four days that I couldn't even get up to accept meal deliveries.

Just like the first episode, I canceled my upcoming plans—several shows, plus my upcoming fortieth-birthday trip to Spain.

I needed a new cardiologist who knew more about pericarditis. My first heart specialist had taken me off the medication and told me to go back to exercise and performance—clearly the wrong call. But I couldn't be certain if this more severe bout was caused by lack of drugs, too much physical exertion, singing, or some combination.

I did know that I didn't want this to happen frequently. Recurrent constrictive pericarditis sometimes requires open-heart surgery to remove scarred portions of the pericardium, leaving the patient vulnerable to more health concerns.

I'm a resilient guy. To be an independent musician for nearly twenty years, you have to pop back up after each knockout punch.

Indie film wants to license your song for $20,000—then it gets cut in the edit. Big rock band wants to take you on tour—then a kid with rich parents buys his band into your place. Life partner is supportive and encouraging—until he's not.

For nearly two decades, I never stayed down. Tour van died. Drummer quit. Partner kicked me out. Touring in blizzards. Playing to just the sound guy. Manager doing nothing. Agent doing nothing. Publicists taking our money to do nothing.

The setbacks just made me want it more—nights on the road with a great audience felt absolutely victorious.

But the piling up of pain and canceled plans threatened to finally keep me on the mat. My fortieth birthday came and went. Instead of living it up on the Mediterranean, I was stuck in my apartment.

Feeling lost, I called my friend Eshanthika back in Chicago for advice. She introduced me to the "Year of Yes" concept. I was told to forget about building my career and just experience life, staying open to possibilities. Most importantly, I was instructed to have sex with men I didn't intend to marry.

I got on Scruff for the first time. I knew I shouldn't meet anyone with the potential for a long-term relationship, so I hooked up with guys who were married and open or who were visiting Nashville. I also started entertaining some of the DMs I got on Instagram, including a hot guy who happened to live where I wanted to go in Spain.

Needing something positive to look forward to, I rescheduled the trip to Málaga for my forty-first birthday.

But after Howard and I met in person, I canceled the trip again so I could spend that week with my best friend.

Howard knew about my plans to go to Málaga, but I didn't tell him when I canceled.

I know it's bad to test your partner, but I just wanted to see how far he would take his openness. After all, this was the man who'd gifted me a copy of *The Ethical Slut* just days after we started talking. Would he ever flat-out tell me to cancel my trip?

He went along with it for months. We had managed to spend about half of our days together from May through October, and we were just trying to figure out when we could see each other in November. I knew my calendar was wide open, but I desperately wanted him to call my bluff.

"Here's the guy I'm staying with in Málaga—and his husband." I showed Howard a photo of two hairy, muscular, bearded gentlemen on a beach.

"No," he scoffed pointedly. He took my phone to look closer.

"No way!" he repeated, handing back my phone. "You're not running off to Spain to fool around with hot Spanish men without me."

I giggled at the "without me" qualifier.

"We can do that next year, but you're not going to Spain by yourself when I don't get enough time with you as it is."

I was still giggling. "I know," I said.

He looked surprised. "You know?"

"Already canceled."

Howard's surprise turned into a warm smile. He got it.

"You're mean," he said. After a moment of deliberation, he added, "My love. How about we take a drive to the Grand Canyon for your birthday?"

If You Want to Sing Out, Sing Out

23

I picked up Howard from LAX on November 6, 2022, and we headed straight to his favorite dispensary. It was a role reversal that I'd been in Los Angeles before him this time.

Howard was coming home from New York, where he attended his friend Dr. Jennifer Ashton's wedding. He wanted me to come with him, but I had a commitment to an organization called Pants Off Racing, which raises money to support families afflicted by pancreatic cancer. It was their annual fundraiser race in Los Angeles. Their founder was a great friend, and I promised to be there to help.

Howard texted me photos over the weekend—the wedding was magnificent, and he looked absolutely dashing in a tux. I regretted not being there with him, but he assured me that we'd have plenty of opportunities to dress up together. We were headed to his cousin's wedding next February in Atlanta, another in Montreal the following July, and of course our own wedding.

With the holidays almost upon us, I was excited for Howard to meet my parents and clear the way for our "happily ever after" here in California. Although we had just signed a lease together in Nashville, we were ready to be done texting each other "good night" and "good morning."

"I want to live together," Howard said when we got back to his house. I carried the two suitcases he'd packed for his weekend trip. "The distance is too frustrating."

I set the suitcases down just inside the door and turned back as Howard closed the door behind him. He looked tired from the trip.

"Me too," I agreed. "I'm setting up our place in Nashville, but I'd rather be figuring out where my stuff goes here."

We spent the next two days doing nothing of note for the first time. It was both ordinary and magical. Then we set out for the Grand Canyon.

A Cat Stevens song came on and reminded me to ask about the French *Harold and Maude* poster I'd noticed hanging in his laundry room. Turns out he had gotten it from his friend, the actor who played Harold.

"Great movie," I said. "We watched it with my AP English class."

"Kind of an interesting plot line, huh babe?"

"Yeah, it's just like you and me," I said, with a wry smile.

Howard scoffed. "Except you're not that young, mister."

"And I need you to go well past eighty." I looked over. Howard was looking out the passenger window.

"I will," Howard assured me. "I've gotta have at least forty years married to you, angel."

In forty years, I'd be turning eighty-one. Howard would be one hundred and six. I pondered the math as the barren desert landscape rolled past.

What a brutal environment. The two-lane road looked like a strip of cracked leather, losing a slow battle with the sun and hot tires rushing to be anywhere but there. The only vegetation able to grow in the endless sea of dirt were cacti and bushes with menacing leaves.

I double-checked my math, and let the numbers sink in. I started thinking about average lifespans. Don't men live to about eighty on average these days? And wouldn't that statistic include tragically young deaths, which would pull that average lower, meaning that otherwise, healthy men are probably making it to around one hundred fairly frequently? Yeah. Howard ate well and exercised.

Sure, he smoked weed, but he didn't drink alcohol. He also had a fancy concierge doctor and any time anything felt even a tiny bit off he went to get checked out. Yeah, I assured myself. If anyone was going to make it past one hundred, it would be Howard.

We stopped at a roadside diner for a late breakfast. The coffee was gas station grade. Howard got out his phone and showed me a picture that made me shudder.

It was a mock-up of his tombstone.

"What the fuck?" I asked a little too loudly.

"Babe, don't worry. I'm going to be living a long, long time," Howard said.

"Then why would you design your tombstone?"

"Because I won't be there, and I don't want anyone to fuck it up!"

He laughed.

I didn't.

We both looked out the window for a time. Just past the parking lot the desert stretched out to meet the horizon. Distant shadowy mountains marked the line between Earth and sky. Howard must've put together where my head was at between our *Harold and Maude* conversation and this morbid revelation.

"Look. I've had some friends go in their fifties and sixties, and I just realized I'm at that age where it's a possibility."

I held his hand but kept looking out the window.

"I'm not going anywhere," he said. "I promise. I promise we'll have forty years together. And then we can pull a *Thelma and Louise*."

"That's a much better movie ending for us," I said somberly, meeting his eyes once again.

The conversation moved on to less morbid subjects—our plans for the Grand Canyon, college football, truck-stop hookups, and the people staring at us as we held hands across the table.

I paid the tab on my way back from the restroom. Sipping the last of my coffee, I stood by our table waiting for Howard to get up.

"However long we get, mister," I said, "I'm glad we found each other."

"Took us long enough," Howard laughed as he scooted out of the booth.

Perhaps it was the vastness of the desert that led us to contemplate our own mortality.

It was a cold and clear night when we arrived at the rim of the Grand Canyon. We had the view to ourselves. Dimly lit by the moon, it looked surreal, like standing too close to a painting to see the frame.

We kissed at the edge of the abyss. Two unlikely lovers, separated in age by twenty-five years. We were illuminated by stars whose light had set out millions of years ago, beginning the journey to us just as the river far below had begun carving through solid rock. It felt like we were destined to meet here eons later.

We headed back to the car. Our age difference didn't feel very significant in the grand scheme of things.

We checked into our room at the Maswick Lodge. By this point I knew to give Howard the side of the bed closer to the bathroom, so he had a straight path if he needed to get up in the middle of the night. This worked for me because I prefer the side by the A/C, both to be chilly and for the white noise.

"I really like being able to say, 'good night I love you' instead of texting it," I said to Howard as he climbed into bed.

"Me too," he replied through a yawn.

There are questions that can't be answered regarding concepts too big to fathom. And then there are practical solutions to very small issues. But maybe if you back up far enough, they become one and the same.

Bosom Buddies

24

After a couple of days at the Grand Canyon, we drove to Sedona. Howard had reserved a spot on a bus tour of the scenic red rock buttes.

We joined ten other tourists and filed into a van with the roof sawed off. While we waited to depart, we got to know the rest of the group. There was a couple behind us from Texas, and a family in front of us from India. In front of them was another family from Los Angeles. Howard and I were the lone homosexuals—which was apparently not evident to the group.

"Are you two father and son?" asked the woman behind us in a sweet Southern drawl.

Howard and I smiled at each other.

"Only on our OnlyFans," he said. I laughed out loud. The couple didn't seem amused.

Our tour guide was a bubbly middle-aged woman, wearing a headset microphone so she could drive while excitedly reciting Sedona facts with the enthusiasm of Kristen Wiig's Target Lady from *Saturday Night Live*.

As we neared lunchtime, she pointed up a steep hill and said, "To your right was the longtime home of Lucille Ball." She then told us stories of how the *I Love Lucy* star was one of Sedona's most famous residents.

Howard leaned over to me and said, "I don't think Lucille Ball ever lived in Sedona." It was loud enough for the whole van to hear.

The bus driver smiled condescendingly at Howard in the oversized rearview mirror. "She did indeed live right there in that house. She had many, many, *many* famous parties that were the talk of the town."

The rest of the tour bus sensed an altercation brewing. The families in front of us turned around to size up Howard. He repeated, "Yeeeeah. I'm fairly certain that Lucille Ball never lived in Sedona."

Our tour driver laughed superiorly. "Well," she said, her voice becoming more authoritative, "I've been guiding tours here for twenty years, and I am certain that that was Lucille Ball's house." We were on the main drag running through Sedona now. "But now it's time for lunch."

She parked the van, and everyone went their separate ways. Howard and I found a bar and grill with a view of the red rocks and ordered a couple of sandwiches. He got his phone out while we waited.

"I'm friends with Lucie Arnaz. I want to ask her if her mom ever lived in Sedona."

I shook my head, smiling. "Of course you know Lucie Arnaz."

"What?!" he said, not looking up. "I'm just curious."

We finished our meal and headed back to the bus. Everyone in the group filed into their same seats. Howard and I followed suit. Once we were in, the driver turned to address the group face-to-face. She cleared her throat, then paused to make sure everyone was paying attention. Her energy was very "junior high teacher who just discovered someone stole the cigarettes out of her purse."

"I was just informed by my *boss* that Lucille Ball's people called our office," she said.

The entire tour bus looked at Howard. There was an implied, "awwwwwww... you're in trouuuuubllllllle." Howard smiled devilishly.

"Apparently Ms. Ball's daughter is upset that we're spreading lies about her mom, who never actually lived in Sedona." She tilted her head back and forth as she mockingly whined the words *never-actually-lived-in-Sedona* directly at Howard. We tried very hard not to laugh.

"So. We're no longer allowed to mention Lucille Ball on our tours," she concluded. And with that, she spun back around and put the van into drive.

"What'd you do?" I whispered as we pulled out of downtown, toward the next lookout spot. Howard turned his palms upward and shrugged.

"What," he didn't whisper back. "Lucie said her mom never lived here. And then she asked the name of the tour we were on. I didn't know it'd get back to us so fast."

Our tour guide's tone on the second half of the tour was markedly less effervescent. She refrained from looking directly at Howard or me.

"I think you broke our tour guide," I said to Howard as she halfheartedly pointed out majestic views of red rock formations.

Something So Right

25

After my birthday, we went to our new rental house in Nashville. There was still much to do to make a household together. I just didn't realize quite how much. Thirteen large boxes waited for us on the porch. Howard had sent clothes and household items, his contributions to round out what I'd brought from my apartment.

We both worked haphazardly, moving from room to room in a chaotic flurry of organization. There was no method to our madness; I cleaned shelves and lined them with paper in the hall closet, then set up my record player and vinyl collection in the living room, then unboxed some kitchen items, then went back to putting toiletries in their places.

Howard did the same as he unpacked boxes of things from the New York apartment he'd recently sold to downsize. He assured me that splitting rent with me in Nashville wouldn't be nearly the financial burden of maintaining a second residence, "to have some space from my ex-husband."

I teased him that people with money could afford the space to be comfortably unhappy in their relationships. The rest of us have to deal with our problems in confinement or just call it quits.

"Is that why you and your ex were engaged for six years?" Howard teased.

"Ooh. Sick engagement burn," I replied. "We were only engaged for four."

We'd both tried couples therapy with our respective exes. We were both loyal, optimistic, hard workers. In the end, those relationships just weren't right. Or maybe they started out right and evolved wrong. A friend once told me that just because a relationship ends doesn't mean it was a failure. I suppose we both learned what we did and didn't need from those previous attempts. All the wrong turns turn out right if you wait long enough.

Each time an unpacking tangent led me through the kitchen, I noticed that my battery-operated salt and pepper shakers and cooking oil cruets—both prized Aldi Finds—had been removed from the counter by the stove. But I discovered a large wooden butcher block cutting board, a stack of vintage cookbooks, and a stone mortar and pestle the size of a bowling ball on the counter.

I stopped and scratched my head quizzically. I had machine-washable cutting boards in the drawer. You can't put a butcher block in the dishwasher. I had worked a long time to afford an apartment that had a dishwasher, and the objective was to never have to wash anything by hand again. And I got recipes on my phone and bought guacamole at the store so I had no use for any of these things.

On the other hand, I used my salt and pepper shakers and my cooking oil daily. I searched the cabinets until I found and restored them to their proper places on the counter. I moved Howard's additions to a cabinet and moved on to the next task.

After the third time I swapped our stuff, I laid in wait around the corner from the kitchen.

"Hey!" I shouted when moments later I caught Howard in the act. He jumped, hand still in the cabinet. He turned to me with a grin.

"Babe, these don't belong out."

"What do you mean? I use them every day."

"Yes dear, but they look like clutter."

"What do you mean? They look fine. And you've got all this other stuff I'll never use on the counters."

I knew better than that. I'd learned in therapy, if you have an issue with something, you raise that point on your own time. Never use your own issue in a response to your partner's issue.

"These are stylish, babe. They're part of the décor. Like set dressing," Howard replied.

And here we go. Our first argument. We're not talking about just my thing now. We've both dug trenches. We were both mostly smiling still, at least.

"Mine are stylish, too!" I pleaded.

"They're just not part of the look." Howard's smile started to fade to frustration.

"But I use them. It'll take me time to pull them out and put them away every day. Why not just leave them on the counter? Your stuff will never get used, but it'll sit there gathering dust."

"Well, when you cook, you get everything out, and when you're done, you put it away, and the kitchen always looks great."

"This is just a form versus function debate. You clearly prefer form. I'm all about function."

"Babe, you function just fine," Howard kidded. He had taken his sugar-free iced tea and lemonade out of the fridge at one end of the long kitchen and poured himself an Arnold Palmer.

"Okay," I said, leaning on the counter all the way on the opposite end. "We can leave it how you want it, but you know that after you leave, I'm just going to put the wood block in the cabinet and bring out my salt and pepper shakers, right?"

"You know," he said, putting his glass down on the counter. "Maybe we shouldn't have rented a house together."

He headed for the living room. As he walked, without facing me, he called, "Maybe I should just go back to L.A. and let you have your own place."

Had I really pierced the armor of the mighty Howard Bragman? I felt awful. I followed him.

"No honey, I love that we did this, it means everything to me."

I hugged him from behind and kissed the back of his head because he still wasn't looking at me.

"And it needs to have your personality in it, so it feels like our place. I get it. When we have people over, it'll look great. I'll leave the butcher block out."

He turned around and hugged me back. "You're so sweet."

"And I'll think about you every time I don't use it." I smiled and leaned in for a kiss. He laughed and pulled away. I didn't let him, squeezing him tightly. "You jerk," he murmured as I forced a kiss on his moving lips. He was smiling again. We both giggled. Our first argument had come and gone quickly, but I'd learned an important detail about Howard.

I hadn't considered that Howard's thick skin was penetrable. Maybe he had given that power only to me.

As I lay in bed that night, I turned to watch him sleep. He was facing me on his side, eyes closed, breathing slowly and deeply. He'd entrusted me with his vulnerability. I wanted to protect him.

Guess What? I Love You
"You stay and find the right words for comforting me"

26

On December 1, 2022—nearly seven months since our first rendezvous—I plopped down into my Spirit Airlines seat and fell asleep before takeoff. I was exhausted.

Driving home from gigs overnight, then catching early flights to see Howard. Slipping out of bed to work for a few hours, then waking up early for our morning stroll. Flying back to Nashville to write and record, then hopping on another plane.

We were cramming so much living into our time together, I thought it might kill me.

Fatigue was manageable, but I worried about my pericarditis. Sleep deprivation seemed to bring on the very specific discomfort in my chest that warned me of a recurrence. Each time I felt that knot between my lungs, it stopped me in my tracks—literally from the way it physically hunched me over, and figuratively from the fear that if it escalated, I'd end up back in the emergency room.

More pain. More bills. More canceled tour dates and wasted album releases. More risk of needing open-heart surgery to remove my scarred pericardium.

My first morning back in Los Angeles, I woke up to an empty bed. After brushing my teeth, I bounced down the stairs to find

Howard in his office—sitting on the edge of the couch, protein shake and coffee mug in front of him, news blasting, earbuds in, talking on the phone, and clipping his fingernails. It was how he usually spent his morning before walking the dogs, except one thing was different: he was completely naked.

He had come a long way from our first breakfast in New York.

"Looking good, mister," I said, grinning.

"Thanks angel," he replied, eyes on the TV.

"Am I rubbing off on you?" I asked, proud that he'd gotten more comfortable with his body.

"Never enough, babe." He took a sip of coffee.

"Ooh, good idea," I said. I went to the kitchen and poured myself a cup.

"Can you feed the children?" Howard called from the office.

"Sure thing," I replied. I put Nacho and Curtis' bowls on the counter and prepared their breakfast. I set Curtis' bowl down and quickly removed my fingers. Then I commenced The Negotiation with Nacho.

I would hear Howard negotiating on the phone in the mornings when we were apart. Now it was my turn to try my luck.

The deal starts by offering Nacho one morsel of food at a time. He would bark at it, sniff it, lick it—anything but eat it. Then we move the bowl, because perhaps it's just not in the exact right position. Then we put Nacho's leash on him and threaten to walk without any food. Then we try ignoring him. At this point, Curtis has wolfed down his breakfast and started to encroach on Nacho's food. This escalates The Negotiation into a three-way ordeal, and the added stress causes Nacho to yap shrilly.

"I've seen you tell Oscar-winning writers to shut the fuck up and listen," I once told Howard as I listened to The Negotiation over the phone. "Yet you can't make your dog eat his food."

Now I felt his pain.

Howard had gotten dressed and entered the kitchen.

"Would you please tell your son that he needs to eat his breakfast so we can go for our walk?"

"If he had my genes, he'd be asking for seconds by now," I said.

I joined Howard at the coffee maker, leaving Nacho snarling, protecting his food, still not eating it.

"Good morning," I said softly, putting my hand on the small of his back, pulling him into me. His belly and mine touched. Curtis barked at Nacho, escalating the standoff.

"Good morning," he replied, and wrapped his arms around me. Both dogs let out aggressive growls, lunging for the dish.

"Heyyy!" we shouted in unison. The dogs separated. Reluctantly, so did we.

"We need to take your kids for a walk," I said, chuckling.

"Our kids," Howard replied.

This was my fourth trip to Los Angeles, and Howard's neighborhood was finally beginning to look familiar. As we approached the hedges surrounding Bob Hope's estate, I asked if it was still for sale.

"Yup," Howard replied. "It's just waiting for you to write that hit so you can buy it."

Despite my exhaustion, the week felt like what I wanted my whole life to be. We were always moving—we worked a lot, we made love a lot, and we made a lot of time for friends. Our social circles increasingly overlapped. As an "us," we were receiving high approval ratings. This was auspicious, considering my parents would finally meet Howard in about two weeks. I knew that they would love him. Love "us."

They needed to, because I was all in, not giving Howard up for anything. The first time we chatted on Scruff, I knew he understood me. Now it was as if he'd written my instruction manual. He often finished my sentences. It was frustrating and astoundingly accurate.

When I visited Howard, I turned his guest room into my office. On this trip, I was mixing an album for a client, mixing an EP for myself, promoting a new single, and building two new websites. With the holidays approaching, I felt pressure to squeeze it all in.

"Babe, we have to get going," I heard Howard call from downstairs. "Lunch with our friends in WeHo."

"Arghhhhhhhhh," I moaned at the top of my lungs.

"What's wrong?"

I could feel the cortisol coursing through my shoulders and neck. A wave of tension radiated up to my jaw, out through my arms, down into my chest. My forehead hurt, and I realized I was clenching my face muscles.

Everyone gets overwhelmed. Everything important gets done eventually. Everyone needs to take breaks. In good times, I know these rational thoughts to be true.

But when I'm stuck in my own head, those tenets are nowhere to be found. *I can't finish this right now* becomes *I'll never do any of the things I want to do with my life, and on my deathbed, I will look back and feel like it was all a waste.*

I lumbered down the stairs and found Howard sitting on his office couch, iPad in one hand, not looking particularly hurried to get out the door.

"You okay, babe?" he asked.

I rattled off a dozen things that I simply had to complete this instant rather than go to lunch.

"Guess what?" Howard said matter-of-factly.

"What?" I sighed. I expected him to impart some knowledge from his career. After all, he had built his own successful businesses, too.

"I love you."

He flashed his broad smile.

I closed my eyes and took a deep breath. The tension began to release.

Had it been anyone but Howard, I would've felt belittled.

But Howard was unlike anyone else. I knew from his tone, from the look in his eyes, from all the ways he told me he respected me, from the setlists of my own songs that he'd written for me—complete with patter notes so I'd touch on my brand pillars—he understood me. He knew I was full of anxiety about making a living, fear of failure, and that self-doubt could turn my mood dark in an instant. And he loved me anyway.

"Why did we rent a house in Nashville again?" I wondered aloud after dinner that night. We were watching an episode of *Fleishman Is in Trouble*, and a commercial had just come on. I reclined on the couch with Howard lying between my legs, resting his head on a pillow he'd set on my chest. His hair smelled like sandalwood shampoo. I draped my arms over his shoulders and aimlessly ran my fingers through his chest hair.

"Because you have more to do there," Howard replied.

"I just love spending the whole day with you," I said.

I was casually touching another man while watching TV and discussing our lives together. If closeted, terrified, naïve, twenty-three-year-old Mike could see me now, he would say for sure that I'd "made it."

"We'll get there," Howard said. "We have all kinds of time."

"Yeah," I said. *Fleishman* was starting back up. This was his niece Lizzy Caplan's new show and we were loving it.

I empathized with Lizzy's character. In a flashback, she was frustrated that she hadn't achieved the position that she deserved at her job. And now she regrets that she never wrote the novel she'd vowed to write after quitting the corporate world. Her character wonders what could've been had she followed her passion.

Okay, I thought. *Message received. I haven't achieved the level of success I want. But I'm still doing it. I'll never have to wonder "what if?" because I'm still going. And miraculously, the journey led me here, with the most remarkable man I've ever met lying on my chest.* I squeezed him and kissed the top of his head.

"I feel so safe in your arms," Howard said.

I'd never felt so important.

This Must Be the Place

The next day we went out to lunch, our last meal before I had to fly back to Nashville. I drove, Howard navigated. We were listening to *Speaking in Tongues* by Talking Heads. We pulled to a stop at a red light somewhere in the valley.

The bright blue sky seemed extra vibrant through my sunglasses. I had two hands on the wheel, and Howard leaned over the armrest, slowly caressing the back of my arm.

"Ooooh, this part right here," he purred. "It's my favorite. So soft."

"Do I need to be worried?" I asked, looking over. He was smiling broadly, with gray sunglasses hiding his eyes. I could see my reflection in them. "You gonna make a dress out of me, Bill?"

"It puts the lotion in the basket."

The light turned green as the sweet and unmistakable intro of "This Must Be the Place" filled the car. It starts with a tight drum pattern, funky synthesizer bass, and chirping guitar chords. After four bars, the iconic Prophet 5 synthesizer flutes come in, with their cute trills and rubbery pitch-bending melody.

I looked at Howard. The song didn't appear to be ringing a bell.

"I don't know if you're into Talking Heads, but I've never really understood this song until I met you," I said.

I could tell he was hearing the words as we drove, because he stopped fondling my tricep flab and put his hand back on his knee. He tapped along in rhythm as he looked out the window.

"I've heard this one, yeah. It's nice."

Another light turned red, and I slowed to a stop as David Byrne sang, "I'm just an animal looking for a home…"

The tip of my nose started to burn, and I scrunched it, trying not to tear up. I reached across and took Howard's hand, pulling it over to my side of the car, resting our clutched hands on my thigh with a gentle squeeze.

Mr. Byrne continued, "Share the same space for a minute or two."

Howard turned to me. I saw him notice me losing control of my emotions. He smiled. I scoffed at my own sappiness.

I tried to sing along:

"And you love me 'til my heart stops. Love me 'til I'm dead."

I couldn't finish the verse. My voice turned warbly, more off-key than usual.

The light turned green. I took my hand from Howard's and wiped tears from my eyes before I slowly accelerated.

"Aw babe," Howard said gently. He caressed the back of my upper arm again, finding the soft spot he liked.

"I'm… I guess I'm just grateful," I said.

David Byrne had completed his lyrics, and now the band was vamping out the rest of the song.

"It took so damn long to find you."

My voice trailed off. I cleared my throat to regain my composure. "I think I'm just getting tired. I want to wake up together all the time."

"We will," Howard reassured me. "Let's meet the parents, get through the holidays, and finish the lease. We'll get married and you'll move out here."

"Sounds like a good plan to me."

If I spoke with God more often, I might have heard laughter.

I've Got My Love to Keep Me Warm

28

December 21, 2022. Atlanta, Georgia. I was participating in my first Hanukkah menorah lighting. As Howard's family sang in Hebrew and lit four of the eight candles from right to left, I soaked in the tradition. It was yet another reminder of how much history preceded my appearance in the book of Howard's life.

Not only was I the latest character in a tome that included six decades of family, friends, and celebrity cameos, but the prequel was five thousand years of history and culture with an entirely unfamiliar language. I wanted it all—the man and everything that he brought with him.

I contemplated my future of loving and learning. I wanted to tell Howard's family how honored I was to become a part of it, and that I was committed to learning about their religion and culture. All I could manage to come up with was something like, "I'm so grateful to spend my first Hanukkah with you all." They graciously accepted their gentile guest.

That night, Howard and I piled into the queen-size bed in his nephew's guest room. This was not an easy feat for two husky men over six foot one, but we were used to cuddling ourselves to sleep. He stroked my chest hair while we talked. That night's conversation turned to our nuptials.

We decided that the wedding needed to be in the Southeast so our families wouldn't have far to travel. We agreed that Olivia Hill had to officiate. And we agreed that the gathering should be classy but casual. Two tuxes and food trucks. We started to drift off to sleep together.

"You know," Howard said, breaking the silence. "You're going to have to propose."

"I will," I said. I had already started rolling around ideas. But he had more to say.

"I never thought I would get married again. After my divorce, I told everyone I know that I was going to be a bachelor for the rest of my life."

I could feel his emotions rising. We had been lightheartedly discussing the merits of food truck cuisine. This tone was much more intentional.

"But when you came along, that changed. You've given me everything I thought I could never have in a partner. And you know I want to spend my life with you." I squeezed the hand that was petting my chest. "I'm all in," he concluded. "I just need to know that you are, too."

"I am," I said. My heart felt ready to burst with love and pride. I wanted to be his husband more than anything. "I want to spend the rest of my life with you, too."

After a moment I added, "You know, as long as you don't fuck it up with my parents."

"Oh babe," Howard said with an easy yawn. "Parents love me."

The next morning, we said goodbye to Howard's family and wheeled our luggage back out to my van, which we'd left parked in the cul-de-sac overnight. I was surprised none of the neighbors had reported a suspicious vehicle.

"Could ya give me a hand with this sofa," Howard drawled creepily as I hopped in the back and he slung his first suitcase up to me. Howard's "Wild Bill" was well-worn yet still enjoyable by this point, like an old flannel shirt.

We departed Atlanta to meet my family for Christmas in North Carolina, a moment that would define our Happily Ever After. Howard and I had been talking about marriage for five of the ten months we'd known each other. If all went well with my parents, I would pop the question officially.

If it didn't—well, I would still be popping the question, it would just make things awkward back home.

My parents live on a big hill, with a steeply sloped driveway that twists and turns through woods. Branches scraped the side of my oversized vehicle as we ascended. I parked the van in my usual spot across from the garage. Howard stepped out and nearly tripped over a concrete rabbit.

"Great place for that," he said with an eye roll.

"I mean, it's not like anyone ever walks over there," I defended my parents. They did have a rather large assortment of small statues and figurines, inside and out. Back in our childhood home in Ohio, they were mostly wolves. I noticed that since they had retired and moved to the mountains of North Carolina, the collection had shifted to bears and bunnies. No idea where they stashed the wolves.

We grabbed several shopping bags of wrapped presents and left our luggage in the van. My parents' Chrismukkah gift to us was a rented cabin nearby, where we could have our own space. Howard had sent his contributions to me in Nashville, and I wrapped them along with mine, signing every one of them, "From Mike/Howard." I texted him a picture of a gift for my Auntie Liz. Howard replied:

> Awww
> We're an "us"

We walked up the path to the house, hands full of presents. I was beaming with pride at making this introduction.

But my chest felt tight. It was that kind of stressful moment that you know is coming but still makes your pulse quicken when the moment arrives. Like suddenly it's your turn to order at a fancy restaurant where everything is hard to pronounce.

Howard was eight years younger than my parents and twenty-five years older than me. Would they be skeptical of our age difference? Would it be weirder if they became friends? They had a lot more pop culture in common than I did; they could talk about seeing the Beatles perform on *Ed Sullivan*, what class they were in when JFK was assassinated, or where they watched the moon landing. What if I felt left out of the conversation?

Another bunny statue greeted us next to the front door. There was also a black bear with a fishing hat, reading a book. This was different than the modern art at Howard's front door—a waist-high bronze sculpture of a hand reaching out of the front stoop. To me, my parents were sophisticated. They took me to the Cleveland Orchestra and art museums when I was young. But Howard produced a documentary on Gustavo Dudamel and owned a Picasso. Would he come off as pretentious? Name-droppy? I didn't think so. But maybe? My sweaty palms told me I was more anxious than I'd thought.

As I rang the doorbell, I saw their dog Nicco through the window, turning in excited circles with his tail wagging. My mom yelled, "Just a minute," as she got up from the couch. She smiled broadly when she came to the door.

"Michael!" she exclaimed, opening the inner door. I opened the screen and stepped inside, nudging Nicco back with my knee. Before I could hug my mom, Nicco hopped up on his hind legs, pawing at my thighs, nearly punching me in the crotch, while whining and barking excitedly. I tried to placate him with head scratches while juggling the presents. Howard came in behind me and put his bags of gifts down. A new person was too much for Nicco, who began to sprint excited laps around the house. I hugged my mom.

"Merry Christmas," I said over the noise of Nicco's stampede. "Mom, meet Howard. Howard, this is my mom."

"So nice to meet you, Howard," my mom said warmly.

"Nice to meet you, Mom," Howard said with a grin.

My mom laughed as they hugged hello. "What a corker," she said. She liked him already.

"Corker?" Howard asked.

"Like a smart ass," I said. "But it's a good thing."

"Just like my Michael," my mom said.

Nicco rounded the corner from the living room, full speed, and took a flying leap at Howard. My parents' dog was not small, but neither was Howard. He withstood the pounce, holding Nicco's two front legs as if they were about to begin a ballroom dance. Nicco nibbled on Howard's hands. I leaned down and hefted Nicco up off the ground, cradling him in my arms. "Be nice to my man," I said. Nicco squirmed but I held onto him.

"Angel, be careful of your heart!" Howard said.

"Yeah!" my mom agreed, escalating the level of concern in the room.

I put Nicco down. "I'm fine you guys," I said. "The cardiologist said I can go back to lifting weights."

By Christmas I hadn't had a pericarditis flare in seven months, but Howard was still concerned about my health.

"Well, I just wish you'd take it easy," Howard said.

"Really Michael, just be careful," my mom took his side.

Howard, my mom, and I went out to dinner. My dad was giving my aunt a ride in from Ohio, and my mom was happy to have the first shot at interrogating Howard all by herself.

We went to a nice restaurant with linens on the table. My mom grew up in a blue-collar household in a working-class neighborhood, but she sure knew a lot about fancy things. Which was perfect, because so did Howard. They compared notes on their childhoods during the automotive golden age—my mom in South Bend, Indiana, and Howard in Flint, Michigan. Then I zoned out while they discussed the British monarchy. Something about a Prince Henry and his wife Meghan? They were eloping and there's a book coming out about it. Or something. I wasn't listening. But they were enjoying themselves, so I happily daydreamed, only mildly disturbed by how much my mom and future husband had in common.

Howard finished his meal first. Our server reached in to clear his plate.

"No thank you, we're not all finished," he said, politely preventing the removal of his empty dish.

The server looked surprised. I grinned at my mom. She smiled.

"I picked a good one, right?" I said.

"Yes," my mom agreed. "This one has manners."

It was one of my mom's biggest pet peeves when waiters took one person's plate early. Howard had unknowingly won a shitload of brownie points with her.

I actually agreed with them, although I'd never stop the plate removal. It isn't a stuffy etiquette thing, it's common sense. It makes the person who finished early feel like a pig, and the people who haven't finished feel like they need to rush.

When the check came, Howard and I both reached for our wallets, but my mom insisted on treating "her boys."

We dropped my mom off at home after dinner. I walked her to the door while Howard headed toward the van across the dark driveway.

"I like him," my mom said as we hugged goodnight. I heard Howard curse as he tripped over the concrete bunny again.

"Me too," I replied. I was so proud.

When it came time to exchange presents, I passed out several that I'd gotten for my family as well as the gifts that Howard had picked out and I'd wrapped.

We sat next to each other on the couch. My mom had the loveseat on Howard's other side, while my dad, his sister, and my sister had their own chairs. In our small family, each person opens one gift at a time while everyone else watches. I've heard that some families have a free-for-all, but the Maimones have a series of presentations.

My dad unwrapped his present from Howard. It was a Nelson Rockefeller book, a small humorous book about Cleveland, and a three-volume biography on Theodore Roosevelt. They chatted briefly about the selections, and my dad concluded with his approval. Howard had officially charmed both of my parents.

It was my turn to give Howard his gifts. He went for the largest box first and methodically removed the paper. I took the resulting large sheet and draped it over Nicco, who was happily gnawing on a new plush toy, trying to remove the squeaker.

Howard removed the white lid. Unfolding the tissue paper, he pulled out a blue throw pillow with white writing. In script were the words, "May I make a suggestion?"

"Hey! My mom always used to say that!" he said, turning to me, surprised.

"I know," I said. "I pay attention."

He had forgotten that he'd told me that story. His mom, like Howard, was infamously forward in a kind way. She always said whatever needed to be said, even if it was tough love. And whenever steering someone back onto the right path, she would preface her directions by asking, "May I make a suggestion?" Apparently, she said it so often that the family talked about having it embroidered on a pillow, but nobody ever made that happen.

He laughed out loud and put his hand on my knee. "Thanks, babe!"

I put my arm around his shoulder. With my other hand I picked up a flat box that looked like it might contain a dress shirt from a department store. He tore the paper off this one excitedly, lifted the lid, and reached under the white tissue paper inside. He pulled out a gold frame housing a hand-drawn sketch.

"Two drifters..." it said in bold, rounded letters at the top. Beneath it was an ink sketch of two men—one with curly hair and a dark beard, the other with neatly trimmed hair and a full salt-and-pepper goatee—holding hands on the banks of a river. A full moon hung above the pair. Words beneath the scene finished the phrase: "off to see the world."

"My friend Shane Sweeney does these lyric drawings," I said, squeezing Howard's shoulder. He held it up so my family could see.

"Very nice," said my aunt. My sister and parents agreed. Howard was quiet. He held the framed artwork with both hands, resting it back on his lap.

"I had him draw it for you," I said softly.

"Angel," he finally said, "I adore this." He turned and looked into my eyes. I could see that he was touched. I leaned in, not breaking eye contact. Close enough to smell his aftershave, I hesitated, smiling mischievously. He raised his eyebrows. "Your move," he intimated silently, playfully. I kissed him softly on the lips.

I couldn't recall whether I'd ever kissed a man in front of my family, but they'd get used to it. Mission accomplished. We had our families' approval, and wedding bells rang in my ears.

What Are You Doing New Year's Eve?

The next day we flew back to Howard's house in Los Angeles. In all our travels that year, we had never flown together. We'd always rendezvoused. Actually, in fifteen years of long-term relationships, not once had I hopped a plane with the man I loved.

I envisioned joining the Mile High Club, but due to our size I assumed the plane bathroom wouldn't do. I contemplated those logistics while waiting in the TSA line. Howard had Clear and was already through security. By the time I met back up with him on the other side, I had concluded that just holding hands together on a plane would be perfect.

There was only one issue. Our seats weren't next to each other. He was across the aisle and one row back.

I sat in my extra-wide first-class seat. It was so luxurious. I looked back at Howard, who was getting situated. I was not used to sitting in this part of the plane and told myself to just be thankful and enjoy the legroom.

But this was still my Year of Yes, dammit. We were celebrating our first holidays together, and I didn't want the magic to end. I hatched a plan.

"Excuse me," I said politely to the woman next to Howard. "Would it be okay if we switched seats, so I can sit next to my husband?"

Howard grinned with approval. I felt like "husband" amplified the necessity of the situation and hoped this woman wouldn't notice our naked ring fingers.

"Well," she said, "that'd be fine, except I really want to sit next to my husband, too." She gestured across the aisle from her, behind me, where a middle-aged man wearing a flannel shirt, jeans, and cowboy boots smiled at us.

"Alright," I said. "We got this." But that pivotal third seat was still empty.

We waited while the entire plane boarded. Just as the flight attendant prepared to close the door, a young woman hustled through. She was breathing heavily, clearly having sprinted to make the connection, and was not in a good mood.

I took a deep breath and turned around slowly once she had taken her seat behind me.

"Excuse me," I said. I explained the game of musical chairs that would lead to her sitting in my seat so that two couples could sit together.

"So let me get this straight." She sounded exasperated. "You four have this plan to sit together, but it all relies on me to cooperate?"

"Um… yes," I said. I braced for bad news.

"Yeah, fine," she said, standing up.

I vacated my seat so she could take it.

The lady next to Howard moved to the spot next to her husband. And as I took my seat next to Howard, the entire first-class cabin and flight attendants burst into applause.

It was my very own real-life romantic movie airport moment. I proudly took my window seat and leaned in for a kiss. "Nice work, babe," Howard said.

On New Year's Eve, Howard cooked prime rib while I made sides and salad. When the ball dropped in Times Square, we kissed.

"Happy New Year, babe," Howard said. "We're going to have an amazing 2023 together."

Howard wrote a similar note in my Christmas card, which now lives permanently in the box with my holiday decorations. Each season I'll rediscover it, treasuring his handwriting while displaying it alongside the current year's cards—shaking my head at the cruel absurdity that fate left his promise unfulfilled.

"Yeah," I agreed, unaware that our one magical holiday season was ending. "I'm excited for it."

You've Got a Friend in Me

I started looking at wedding bands during my flight back to Nashville on January 11, 2023.

Howard loved Hopi jewelry; he had been on a quest to find the perfect piece during our trip to the Grand Canyon for my birthday. I found some turquoise and silver rings that I thought looked good.

Or maybe we should go with plain black bands. I liked that look. Very masculine. But I couldn't imagine it on Howard.

For a moment I wondered if he'd be into getting wedding tattoos.

I started to sweat from thinking about purchasing jewelry for Howard. Maybe I should just pop the question without a ring, and then we could pick out what we want together.

When the plane landed, I had settled on that plan.

I would do it on his birthday—exactly one year from our first Scruff chat. After his cousin's wedding in Atlanta we were spending three weeks in Puerto Vallarta, hosting a rotating cast of guests at a villa he'd rented. We'd be in Mexico, surrounded by friends, and my official proposal was sure to be magical.

That gave me just three weeks to find Howard's perfect birthday gifts and finish my new album. It would be a stretch.

Then my San Diego singer/songwriter client called, asking if I had any availability to record five new songs for her.

I weighed it out. Money was tight after the holidays and now spending January working on my album and February in Mexico. I needed the gig. But time was also tight. I told her I could do it, but I could only give her three days. It would be rush pricing, but I wouldn't sleep; she could record during the day and I'd edit at night. She agreed to the budget, and before I knew it, I was back on a plane to the West Coast.

Before boarding, I got a text from Howard with a YouTube link. It was his new interview on Robert Black's *Sexual Heroes* podcast. I downloaded it to watch on the flight.

Some of it was familiar. Moving to Chicago and having a few different jobs before finding his passion for PR. Wanting to start his own company that spoke out for gay rights and AIDS awareness while also representing mainstream clients (and not telling his mentor, "I told you so" when he succeeded).

But there was so much more that I hadn't heard, starting with something I wish I could unhear. He opened the interview by thanking Robert for having him, because he "wasn't a young man anymore" and he wanted to "God forbid the word, memorialize his legacy."

When I heard those words, a chill ran through me.

I shrugged it off as probably nothing. After all, even when he showed me his own tombstone mockup, he assured me that he intended us to have forty years together.

He continued to talk about his career. The host asked him about the celebrities he had helped guide out of the closet. This was the first time I heard him discuss his work with Chaz Bono in depth. I knew that he was one of Howard's clients, but I didn't realize how involved he was—even going toe-to-toe with Cher about taking the story public. She wanted Chaz to keep it private. But with Howard's help, it became a formative moment for the trans community.

And Cher soon realized the significance.

When Chaz appeared on *Dancing with the Stars*, Cher asked Howard to sit next to her. He interpreted that as her way of saying, "You were right. I'm glad we did this publicly. It was important."

I paused the interview.

If Howard sat next to Cher at a taping of *Dancing with the Stars*, there had to be footage of them in the audience.

I needed this footage for two reasons.

One, it finally clicked just how remarkable my soon-to-be fiancé was. I knew he worked with celebrities, but I hadn't paid much attention to it. I loved him for how he made me feel. Eating together at home felt more important than meeting his famous friends at fancy restaurants.

But there are very few one-name people on this planet—Cher, Oprah, Prince, Shaq—and my fiancé was hanging out with one of them on national TV.

The second reason I needed the footage is that my mom loved *Dancing with the Stars*. For the first several seasons, I could not get through a phone call with her without at least one reference to the latest episode of *"Dancing."* She already loved Howard from their meeting at Christmas. It thrilled her that he later asked her opinion before appearing on the BBC to weigh in on Prince Harley's situation. This was going to send her through the roof!

I paid the stupid fee for the plane Wi-Fi. Google told me what season Chaz was on. I realized that my heart was pounding. I opened YouTube and searched for "Dancing Season 13 Cher." I had butterflies in my stomach. Several thumbnails appeared.

This was an event that happened over a decade ago, yet I was on the edge of my seat as if the Cleveland Browns were lined up to kick a game-winning field goal.

I found a title that looked promising. It was from ABC News, "Dancing with the Stars: Cher Cheers Chaz Out of Last Place; Ricki Lake Earns 10s." I didn't know yet that the back half of that title would soon be significant. Robin Roberts introduced the segment. I also didn't know how significant that would be. And then, there it was. It was quick. I hit pause and rewound.

When the camera panned the audience for Cher's reaction after Chaz's dance, there was Howard, beaming from the seat next to her. Wow. Wow! He looked radiant on camera. I took a screen grab.

Smiling like a lovestruck idiot, I opened the photo editor on my phone. I found a heart sticker and put it around Howard's face like a thirteen-year-old with a copy of *Bop* magazine.

I texted Howard:

> How's my accomplished man? Great interview mister

> Thanks sweetheart
> You're my proudest accomplishment
> Having you at my side

> Awww
> That means a lot from a man who sat next to Cher at Dancing With the Stars!

> Ha

I sent the screen shot of Howard and Cher applauding, grinning from ear to ear, with the neon heart around Howard's face.

> Found you 😊
> You're so handsome

> Awwwww

Then I sent it to my Mom. And waited...

She never has her phone on.

I texted it to my Dad and told him to show my mom. He said that she remembered that season.

As it turns out, both of my parents had seen Howard on TV before they knew who he was. My dad saw Michael Smerconish interview him on CNN months earlier—the same morning I called to tell my parents I had a new long-distance boyfriend.

I touched down in San Diego and quickly set up a mobile recording studio in my client's living room. Time was of the essence, so we had to move fast. I had just five days until my February adventure with Howard, and I had to wrap up the tracking on this EP, fly back to Nashville, mix this EP, finalize my album mixes to send for mastering, and pack to be away from home for a month. I was feeling a panic attack coming on when Howard's name popped up on my phone.

I needed his positive energy, and my client wasn't ready to record yet, so I took the call.

"Angel," Howard said. He sounded tired. I immediately switched from needing support to giving it.

"Yeah honey, what's going on? Everything okay?"

"I'm heading to the dentist. My gums are really swollen."

"Oh no," I sighed.

"And I'm exhausted. I've been sleeping a lot but I'm worn out."

"I'm so sorry, honey," I said. "I wish there was something I could do. Can I GrubHub you some food or anything?"

I wished I could be there for him. The distance wasn't acceptable anymore. It was exciting to meet up all over the country for a year, but it was time to cohabitate. I wanted to wake up with Howard every day—and to tend to him when he didn't feel well.

"I don't think I can eat right now," Howard said slowly. My stomach sank, the helplessness a rock in my gut.

"Alright, well, let me know what the dentist says, and if you change your mind..."

We hung up the phone and I got back to work. On breaks, I thought about my man driving himself to doctors when he didn't feel well. It wasn't right.

That evening I texted to check up on him.

> Call before bed honey
> Love you

> I'm gonna crash
> So exhausted lover

It was unlike Howard not to hop on the phone before bed. I was a little worried, but I didn't want to let on, so I just typed:

> OK good night, miss you love

The next morning, as I waited for my client to pick me up at my hotel, Howard texted me:

> When you have 5 minutes
> I need to talk to you sweetheart

He had never prefaced a call before. He always just called. I dialed him immediately.

"I will let you out of this relationship to find a younger man," he said, cutting to the chase. He sounded tired, but his voice didn't waver.

"What are you talking about?" I was confused.

"You're a young man. You shouldn't be tending to an old guy."

He was serious.

"Howard, stop."

"Listen. I love you so much. Believe me, it would suck. But I'd survive. I'd rather know that you're happy with someone your own age than see you stuck with…"

"Howard!" I was getting mad. "You're my forever guy! I'm not just going to run away if things get tough. That's not the kind of person I am."

My chest tightened. My mind raced. What was going on?

"Thank you, angel. I love you so much."

We hung up the phone. I was stunned. I wanted to call back. But I'd see him soon and had to get back to work.

A few hours later, my client needed another break. I sketched out some ideas on guitar and bass. When I finished, she still hadn't returned. My mind turned to Howard.

> How is my man?
> Hope you're getting rest.

> Yes. Eating soft food then chilling

> OK good honey. Love you

> I will let you out of this relationship to find a younger man.
> That's how much I love you

> Noooooooooo!

> I love you that much

> I can't picture my life without you. I'm not going to run away just because things aren't easy every single second

> You have a hero's heart. That said, I decline your offer to "let me out."

> I do not let myself out
> I am in

I found a "Put me in, coach!" GIF and sent it.

> You made me cry

The Best

31

Time ran out on recording in San Diego before we could finish.

This singer/songwriter client was creative, but still a novice guitar player. Session players performed on her recordings before she hired me to produce her. It had taken her six hours on the first night to finish one acoustic guitar track, but she was adamant that she played it herself.

I encouraged her, having been there before. Working in studios as a young keyboardist, I discovered that artists commonly had session players cut their album tracks, even though they were good enough to perform them live. I always pushed back on this, even as I got gigs replacing other keyboardists' parts on their own records.

Now that I was in the producer's chair, I empathized and worked with my client to develop parts that she could play and sing consistently. It was time-consuming.

By the time I left California, we just had the bones of three new songs. I turned her two other voice memo ideas into interludes, tying together one cohesive collection. But we hadn't gotten to several of the overdubs we needed. The EP would require a lot more work than I had hoped.

I flew back to Nashville on Tuesday, January 31. I barely slept. The next day I got up early, still haunted by Howard's offer. I checked in with him. He was tired. But he sent me an article about one of my favorite bands OK Go winning a lawsuit that Post cereal had brought against them. Howard's grassroots PR campaign was successful for the indie pop rockers. I congratulated him, thanking God for some positive news. Just two more days until we'd meet in Atlanta for the wedding, and everything would be fine.

I re-recorded my cover of "The Best," which Howard had requested for my mixtape album. This was my third stab at it. It hadn't felt emotional enough yet. Before hitting record on the vocal, I pulled up a photo I took of Howard standing in front of the Grand Canyon. With my eyes on Howard and his health on my mind, I finally got a take that I felt captured the depth of my love for him.

I periodically checked on him via text, and he replied each time that he was still exhausted, resting, and couldn't talk.

That night, Wednesday, February 1, I got a call from my client. She had met with her accountant, who brought to her attention how much she was spending on her music. She was firing me because we hadn't gotten enough done in our most recent session. I was shocked and defended my work. I had put a lot of creative input into the sessions, and if she wanted someone else to finish them cheaper, they were either going to steal my intellectual property and take credit for it, or ruin a really cool EP.

She pushed me, saying that I was inefficient. I reminded her of how long it took to record the initial guitar for the first song. She took offense. The argument escalated. I didn't want to lose this project; I felt great about my work as a producer, and after working with her on two EPs, this third one seemed like it could be a breakthrough for her as an artist.

I finally acquiesced to mixing her three songs for the price of two, not charging for her musical interludes, and comped ten hours of pre-production that I had already done remotely to prepare her for the session. She insisted that she couldn't spend any more money on the recording, and that I had to make it work with what we had already done. I hung up the phone feeling unappreciated and exhausted.

On Thursday, February 2, 2023, I woke up early. I had yet to start packing for tomorrow's trip and I still had a few more mixes to tweak on my album. The music had to be finished so I could do all the non-studio album stuff while we traveled—the album art, ordering CDs and vinyl, publishing and copyright registrations and other administrative work. It was overwhelming, and I doubted I could get it all done. I rushed around the house, a blur of stress.

Around 1 p.m., Howard called. I was in the kitchen, ready to unload everything I was dealing with.

"Hey mister," I started. But I could tell from Howard's breathing that something was wrong. It stopped me cold.

His voice trembled as he said, "Honey, I need you here." He paused.

"It's leukemia."

He broke into sobs.

My mind went blank.

Wait. What?

My head spun.

I struggled to stand.

I braced myself on the countertop.

Isn't leukemia… cancer?

This couldn't be happening. Not to my giant bear of a man. My best friend. My soon-to-be husband.

My Howard has cancer?

I needed to be with him. I told him I was changing my flight and I'd be there tonight.

"Not tonight," he replied. "Tomorrow is fine."

He was at Cedars-Sinai Hospital and confidence was high with his team, who were doing tests to determine which type of leukemia he had. I was worried, and he could tell.

"I'm not going anywhere," he assured me.

It was my turn to cry. I had started picturing the rest of my life with Howard. We were just getting started. He absolutely could not go anywhere.

I threw what I thought I'd need into a suitcase. Howard would receive a round of chemo, and although we'd miss the Atlanta wedding, he told me we might be able to get to Mexico for a week. In went the Speedo that he bought me—that I would only ever wear in front of him. In went a couple of jockstraps, which again, I never wore on my own but I knew he liked. In went my travel keyboard and mixing headphones. And in went the gifts I had gotten for Howard's birthday, which I planned to give to him, then drop to a knee and propose in front of our friends.

I'm not sure if I slept. I kept picturing Howard in a hospital bed, all alone. When morning mercifully came around, I texted him:

On the plane I bought the Wi-Fi again so I could research leukemia. It turned out there are four types—three of which have promising survival rates. But one did not. I begged God, "Please not AML." As the plane descended into Burbank Airport, I noticed how green the mountains were around the San Fernando Valley. It was golden hour, and the majestic scenery gave me hope. This was going to be okay.

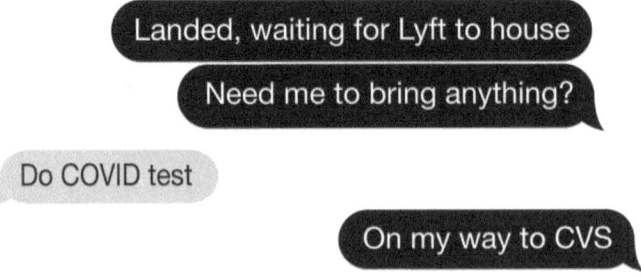

The Best

I took Howard's car to the nearest CVS and frantically paced the aisles looking for the COVID tests. My head seemed to have disconnected from my body. All I could think about was Howard in a hospital bed by himself. I needed to plug my brain in and get to him. I grabbed a test, checked out, drove home, tore open the package, assaulted my nostrils for the thousandth time, watched fifteen excruciating minutes pass by on my phone timer, and then got back in the car.

> They brought my food

>> OK
>> If it sucks let me know, I'll bring you something else

> Not hungry
> I have lemonade and cookies for you

>> Yay!

I followed my phone's directions to the hospital, driving as patiently as possible through Los Angeles traffic. It seemed like there were more people on the road at 7 p.m. on a Friday night than lived in my entire hometown.

I parked in the first parking lot I saw, in front of the Steven Spielberg Pediatric Research Center. I did a double-take at the name before remembering that I was in Hollywood. I was frazzled and unable to see clearly, much less think clearly. I darted toward the place I thought the front door would be given the address was on Beverly Boulevard. Nothing. I walked all the way around the massive building.

>> Sorry I have no idea how to get in do you know what street the entrance is off of?

I found what looked like the main entrance. But the door was closed and locked, no lights on at the front desk.

It felt like it was taking as long to get from Howard's house to his hospital room as it took to get from Nashville to L.A., and I was about to throw my phone as far as I could out of frustration.

I stood in the ambulance entrance, debating running in the door marked for hospital personnel only. Instead, I called Howard's cell. He put me on the phone with a nurse, who guided me to where I needed to be. I breathed a sigh of relief, put on my face mask, and ran inside—only to encounter a long line of other concerned family members waiting to check in.

I hung up the phone, breathing heavily, heart pounding, sweating, until I was finally called up to the desk. The attendant checked my ID, printed a wristband, and pointed me toward the elevators.

At last, I made it to his room.

I saw Howard before he saw me. He was talking to his nurse from behind a yellow face mask. This was bizarre. I had taken Howard to doctor's appointments, Urgent Care, even picked him up after knee surgery, but I had never seen him in a hospital gown.

He seemed... fine. It shouldn't have surprised me. No matter where he was, Howard was Howard.

I walked into the room. When he saw me, his eyes lit up.

"Hey babe," he said. "Say hi to Brad."

His nurse and I introduced ourselves.

"Told you he was hot," Howard said to Brad. I shook my head.

Other than the hospital gown, he was my Howard.

I leaned over his bed and kissed the side of his head through my mask. He had a five o'clock shadow, which was unusual, though I liked that look on him. Brad smiled at me and returned to his charts.

"Thanks for getting here so fast," Howard said. I assumed this was half genuine and half making fun of me for not being able to find the entrance. "Hungry? Have my cookies and lemonade."

He knew I was always hungry when I traveled. I sat next to him on the edge of his bed, calming down as I ate. My heart finally stopped pounding. Even in a hospital bed, Howard's mere presence was calming. I put my hand on his thigh.

Looking around the sterile room, it finally sank in that this was really happening. My head started to spin. Howard's calm and steady voice snapped me out of it.

"I'm going to beat this," he said, resting one hand on mine. There was an IV line taped neatly to it. I took a deep breath.

"Of course you are," I said.

"But this is going to be the fight of my life, and I need you to be my husband to get through it."

When couples promise, "in sickness and in health," it's usually hypothetical—but my vow was already very real. I flashed forward through everything I'd heard about long battles with cancer: years of chemo, remission, hope, recurrences, frustration, hospital stays, and endless doctor's appointments. A proposal meant committing to becoming Howard's husband and caretaker—seeing him through all of it. Things would never be the same as our fairytale first year together.

"Howard Bragman," I said, taking his hand in mine. "Will you make me the luckiest man alive and be my husband?"

"Yes, my sweet angel," Howard replied.

I pressed my mask against his and kissed my new fiancé's lips through two layers of medical fabric.

This was not the proposal I'd been envisioning for months, but our engagement was finally official.

Beautiful Mess
"Heaven help, if you can"

32

On Friday night, February 3, 2022, I carried Howard's brown leather backpack and a clear hospital bag with his clothes toward the oncology floor. This was really happening. I didn't know what to say. Howard seemed composed, but maybe he was in shock, too. We stayed silent as we followed the medical professionals into the unknown.

Another nurse waited for us outside Howard's new room. He introduced himself and told me that this is where we would be until Howard was healthy enough to go home. I mentally buckled in for the ride.

The transport wheeled Howard's bed into place with a sixteen-point turn. It was no small feat to maneuver—Howard required an extension to accommodate his tall frame. The medical staff traded information, wrote notes on the whiteboard, and I unpacked Howard's things.

"This will do," Howard said, lowering his mask. He seemed comfortable in his bed, not the least bit worried.

"Do for what?" I said through my mask as I slipped his notecards and papers out of his backpack and into his nightstand drawer. He planned on working from his hospital bed.

"Our Super Bowl party," he said. "We'll put the catering trays on that wall, we'll bring in some chairs and our guests can sit right there." He motioned to the small open area between himself and the bathroom, currently occupied by four hospital staff, in front of the mobile computer stand and other equipment.

The Super Bowl was in nine days. I pictured the two of us watching snuggled up in his bed, eating wings, laughing at the commercials together, Howard using his eagle eye for pointing out VPL. He made it sound fun, like a sleepover at a friend's house. I felt a wave of optimism wash over me as I emptied the rest of his backpack.

And then I noticed a sheet of white paper with handwriting in black marker. At the top it said "A.M.L. - Acute Monocytic Leukemia," followed by what looked like the first treatment steps.

The optimism vanished as I remembered the graph I had seen comparing five-year survival rates of the four main types of leukemia. Three were over seventy-five percent. AML was closer to twenty percent. I didn't want to tell him. I wanted to unsee that fucking statistic myself. If anyone could beat odds like that, it was Howard. Stats didn't apply to remarkable people like him.

Saturday, February 4, 2023. The next morning, we met with the oncology team and Dr. Gary Cohan, the primary physician who had made the initial diagnosis.

Once we were alone, Howard laid out the plan for breaking the news to friends and family. We were missing his cousin's wedding in Atlanta that day, but he didn't want to ruin the celebration. He had only told his brother, asking him to inform the rest of the family that Howard was absent due to COVID. Then he texted the Puerto Vallarta group, insisting they still go to the villa he'd rented, and that we'd be there as soon as possible.

Following Dr. Gary's advice, we set up a CaringBridge page—a central website to update everyone on Howard's recovery.

Dr. Gary's other suggestion was more difficult to fulfill. I was supposed to commandeer my new fiancé's phone so that he would rest. I couldn't picture Howard relinquishing his phone under any condition. It was his lifeline. The man communicated with more people in a day than I did in a month.

But that afternoon he handed me his phone, and we began the project of informing his friends of his condition.

We couldn't tell anyone who would be at the wedding, and he didn't want to alert the whole world. This ruled out a social media post; we would have to be more selective.

I pulled my oversized sleeper chair close to Howard's bedside and went down the list of his recent texts one by one, reading out names.

As I read each one, he said "Yes," "No," or "Not yet." For each affirmative, I pasted our announcement with the CaringBridge link, changing the greeting to the correct first name. It occurred to me that I was helping Howard Bragman, the preeminent crisis management publicist, do his own crisis management PR.

Responses began pouring in. I tried to keep up. I read the words of encouragement to Howard, who dictated responses to me. I found out later that many non-responders assumed this was a phishing scam.

After several hours, we were both exhausted. I crawled into bed next to him. He had shed the hospital gown and facemask, opting for a tank top and shorts. He received oxygen through a clear plastic tube in his nose. An IV in his hand connected him to another machine. I kissed his cheek through my mask, and he rolled onto his side.

"Thanks for doing all that, babe," he said as I put my right arm over his shoulder. My left arm fit perfectly in the tunnel between his shoulder, neck, pillow, and mattress.

"This okay? I'm not squishing you, am I?"

"No, angel."

I got as close to Howard as I could, taking care not to disturb the cables attached to him.

"Babe," Howard said, starting to doze. "We make a good team."

I listened to him breathing slowly as he slept. I had a feeling Howard would make it through this. We would get married in one of the conference rooms next week and have a party for family and friends in the summer. We would celebrate Howard for beating cancer even more than we celebrated our nuptials. I followed him to sleep, my face just inches from the back of his head, listening to the steady beep of hospital equipment, and promising myself that I'd never forget the way his hair smelled.

I woke up slowly sometime later. Before opening my eyes, I felt my arms around Howard in the comfort of our own bed. I smiled and squeezed him gently.

Then I heard the unmistakable beeping of hospital equipment nearby. I noticed voices farther away. Disoriented, I opened my eyes, and the nightmarish reality came rushing back—bed rails, a curtain, oversized hospital doors, tubes in Howard's arm and nose.

He yawned, and I gave him room to roll onto his back. I knelt above him, one hand on either side of his head, one knee on either side of his waist. His eyes snapped into focus on mine. He smiled and whispered, "Good morning, my angel."

Dusk had filtered through the window, casting the peach walls in a cool blue. Time has no relevance in a hospital. I kissed him on the forehead through my mask.

"That was a really nice nap."

"Yeah," he agreed. "I forgot where we were for a bit."

I felt a hand exploring up my shirt.

"Howard," I said. "I'm not sure we should..."

"I need to touch your skin," he said.

"You can have whatever you want, honey," I said. "But look what else you're waking up."

Howard's eyes widened and he tilted his head to look down. He slid his hand out from under my shirt and down my gym shorts, flashing a mischievous grin.

The oncology team and Dr. Gary entered the room with a quick knock. Startled, I rolled onto my side and sheepishly tried to hide my arousal with my arm.

The doctors informed us that Howard's white blood cell count had spiked to over 100,000—an alarming number considering normal levels range between 4,500 and 10,500. He needed a treatment called leukapheresis to physically remove white blood cells from his blood. This entailed inserting a central line, drawing his blood out, filtering it through a machine, and then returning it to his body. In his compromised condition, the procedure would be perilous, so we needed to move to the ICU.

"What the fuck?" I said, trembling, looking back and forth between Howard and the doctors. I felt cold. I was positive that ICU were three letters we didn't want to hear. I was terrified.

Howard reacted as if he were scheduled to work out with his personal trainer.

"Let's get this over with," he said.

I started packing up Howard's things, the pit in my stomach growing by the second. The transport arrived several dreadful moments later, and our once-tranquil room was now filled with a medical team preparing Howard for the move. A nurse placed a battery-powered machine on the bed by Howard's waist. The team systematically detached the tubes and wires from Howard's oxygen mask, blood pressure cuff, IV, and heart monitor leads, re-connecting them to their battery-operated equivalents for transit. They directed me to put Howard's clothes on the bed. Apparently, we had a long way to go, and we were using Howard's extra-long bed as a moving truck, too.

The transport carefully maneuvered Howard and his bed full of personal belongings and medical devices out of the room and down the hall, flanked by nurses. I started to follow, but the oncology team and Dr. Gary pulled me aside.

"He'll be right there, Howard," Dr. Gary called down the hallway.

"We just want to clarify what's going on," said one of the oncologists. The two main doctors that I had seen were both young. One male, one female. Neither looked old enough to have been alive when I drank my first legal beer. I remembered my Auntie Liz once saying, "When did they start letting children get medical degrees?" I finally understood the alarm it caused.

The oncologist assured me that the move to the ICU was precautionary. This was an intense procedure, but a relatively routine one. Because of Howard's weakened condition, they just wanted the best resources available at the remote chance that something should go wrong. After this, they insisted, he'll be back up in the oncology wing, and they saw a clear path forward to recovery.

Tears welled up in my eyes. I took a deep breath and stood up straight. The relief made me realize that every muscle in my body had been clenched.

"Thank you guys," I said as the oncologists walked toward the elevators.

I turned to follow, but Dr. Gary once again pulled me by my elbow. Without speaking, he motioned to hang back.

"Mike," he said, once the cancer team was out of sight. "I want you to be careful here."

I started to reply that I understood, but he continued pragmatically, "Howard is a tough son of a bitch, and we have an incredible team of doctors here. But they're not going to give you the full picture." His bloodshot eyes contradicted his calm demeanor. It looked like he hadn't slept in days.

Comeback Story

Dr. Gary and Howard had been friends since the '80s. They had endured the AIDS epidemic together—Gary in the hospital and Howard as an advocate with AIDS Project Los Angeles, raising awareness and funding for research. There is a bond among LGBTQ+ people who survived the trauma of that era that few can fully comprehend. They watched loved ones die tragically. They cursed their government for refusing to come to their rescue. They tended to each other when nobody else would. Howard and Gary were like war brothers.

I didn't know Gary, but my intuition told me that he knew what he was talking about, and to trust that his level of concern was the correct one.

That said, I desperately wanted to believe the young doctors about their "path forward." I'm from Cleveland. We don't know how to give up hope.

He must've read this on my face. He said, "Yes, you need to be his rock. Be by his side, stay optimistic, and hope for the best." He paused, not breaking eye contact. "But I just want to make sure somebody is here to manage your expectations, because this is not as simple as they're letting you believe. This is a med school final exam case. Every system in Howard's body is failing. And when we try to fix one, it affects the others."

I nodded that I understood. My chest had tightened and I realized I hadn't been breathing. I forced myself to take a deep breath and we started down the long hall toward the elevators.

"You know," Gary added, "he didn't want to come in for testing."

"What do you mean?" I asked, looking at the floor as we walked.

"I practically dragged him into my office. He was so annoyed with me. All he wanted me to do was prescribe something over the phone to get him to Atlanta and Mexico with you. He told me you were going to make your engagement official when you got there."

"Wow," I said, shocked. "He read my mind."

In the elevator, Gary pressed the button for the ground floor, and I got lost inside my own head.

Fine, so I had to temper my hopefulness—but what does that look like in practice? How does a person hold a loved one, tell him it's going to be okay, and mentally prepare for the worst at the same time?

I seemed to watch myself following Gary outside, across a courtyard, and into another building.

At the check-in desk I showed my ID and was issued a new badge. By the time we got up the elevator and stood waiting for someone to let us into the ICU, I had decided to forget about "managing my expectations" and go full force with "be his rock."

We crossed through the middle of the ICU and found Howard's room. He had already gotten his main line. I was shocked to see a valve protruding several inches from his neck.

"Like Frankenstein's monster, huh babe?!" Howard said playfully, flashing a great broad smile.

Howard never seemed in need of a rock to stand on, but I vowed to be there in case he ever did.

He asked me to unpack his clothes from the plastic hospital bags into the drawers along the far wall. Every time we stayed in a new room—whether on a road trip or in a hospital—the first thing he wanted to do was unpack and get settled.

The ICU nurse, a neatly groomed young man, entered the room.

"Chris," Howard said, "this is my fiancé, Mike. Mike, meet Chris."

"Hey Chris," I said.

"Nice to meet you, Mike," said Chris.

"'Fiancé' feels good, doesn't it?" I said to Howard, squeezing his hand in mine. He agreed, then proceeded to tell me where Chris grew up, where he went to school, that he was single, looking for a long-term boyfriend, and saving up to start his own business. Chris smiled as he worked.

"You got it all, Howard!"

Aside from settling into each new room, Howard interviewed each new nurse about his or her life story. And he remembered every detail—he wasn't just being polite, he was innately curious and considerate of people's motivations, interests, and well-being. The world is an infinitely vast novel, and Howard devoured as many pages as he could.

Sunday, February 5, 2023. Most of the ICU was composed of stalls with their curtains pulled open, so I could see the other patients as I returned to Howard's room the next morning. Everyone had their eyes closed. Some had skin that appeared cold and caked on like dried clay, with their mouths hanging open. They seemed to be in a completely different condition than Howard. *He doesn't belong here,* I reassured myself, *he's going to be fine.* I spent the rest of the walk reciting Hail Marys in groups of ten, separated by an Our Father and a Glory Be—decades of the rosary for Howard and the other ICU patients. And then I apologized for only praying when I needed something.

When I reached the room, a tech was setting up the leukapheresis machine. The procedure began—withdrawing Howard's blood, cleaning it, and then putting it back. The sound of gears and pumps whirring and clicking methodically would've been soothing like white noise, had it not been accompanied by the sight of Howard's blood flowing through a series of tubes.

I sat in a chair pulled up against the opposite side of Howard's bed, holding his hand. He lay almost flat—a position he insisted helped him breathe better. He wore nothing but boxer briefs and an oxygen mask; they'd removed his tank top to attach heart monitors to his chest, which we had successfully petitioned the nurses not to shave. Wires crisscrossed his body. He looked straight up at the ceiling. His complexion paled, his energy dropped, and his voice—ordinarily booming effortlessly—became very hushed.

"Does it hurt?" I asked, wincing.

"It doesn't feel good," he murmured from behind his oxygen mask.

"Don't talk," the tech said. "You're going to loosen the line."

Howard rolled his eyes.

"So thirsty," he whispered, looking to me without moving his head. He hadn't been allowed water all day in preparation for this procedure.

"Can he have a sip of water?" I asked the tech.

"No," she said flatly. She didn't look up, continuing to watch her machine and write notes on a clipboard.

"Maybe some ice chips?"

"Not a good idea."

No sympathy from this one. The procedure continued, and time slowed to a crawl.

Howard lifted his oxygen mask slightly, cables cascading from his arm as he moved. "Ice chips," he whispered. It sounded like his tongue had been replaced with sandpaper. "Throat dry."

"Can we please let him just suck on an ice chip?" I implored the tech.

She let out an exasperated sigh and relented. "Just a tiny bit."

I pressed the call button and the tech helped me elevate the head of Howard's bed. In a few moments we were given a large clear plastic cup filled with ice chips. I washed my hands, stood by Howard's bed, and picked up a small flake of ice, placing it in his mouth.

"Just let it melt," the tech said. "No sucking." Howard winked at me weakly. I smiled, relieved that he still had his sense of humor despite his discomfort.

"One more," he whispered when the first one had melted. I obliged, holding my breath in anticipation until it had safely disappeared.

"Okay I think that's good," I said, nervous about pushing our luck.

"Just one more," Howard whispered. I looked at the tech. She was shaking her head disapprovingly.

"Please, angel?" Howard asked.

What could I do? I set another ice chip on Howard's tongue.

As it melted, Howard began to choke.

"DO NOT COUGH!" the tech shouted, jumping out of her chair to steady the valve that was now in jeopardy of shooting out of Howard's neck.

"Breathe through your nose," I begged Howard. "Just relax your throat and breathe through your nose."

His eyes widened as he stifled his cough. His face turned red. He held his breath, veins appearing in his neck and forehead. He tried to sit up straight. The tech stopped him.

"DON'T MOVE!" she ordered.

Howard couldn't hold it in anymore. He coughed. Blood spurted from his valve, splashing onto his chest and the white pillowcase.

"STOP MOVING!" The tech shouted, holding the valve in place. "You're losing blood!"

"I haven't lost it!" Howard growled back, tired of being told what to do. "It's bright red! Look, it's right there!" He pointed at the splatter on his upper chest. Then he noticed spots on the bedsheet. "And there!"

The tech was not amused.

Howard relaxed. "One more," he said softly.

"NO!" said the tech.

"I think you're done for now, mister," I sighed, placing the cup on his bedside table.

A couple of hours passed, and the procedure was complete. The tech packed up her machine and rolled it out of our room. I thought I detected a touch of "good riddance" in her gait.

We were alone once again. Howard looked exhausted, like he'd just run a marathon followed by a heavyweight boxing match. Dried blood had caked around his main line, and I noticed that he had developed bruises on his hands and arms. I handed the cup of melted ice chips to Howard and he chugged the frigid water in about two seconds.

"That was incredible," he gasped, eyes sparkling. His dinner arrived on a plastic tray. I put a straw in the small plastic pitcher of water and gave it to him. He drank feverishly, exclaiming hoarsely in between pulls, "This is the most delicious thing I've ever tasted." He drank so fast he was out of breath. I rang the nurse's station for more water. Several refills later, Howard's thirst was finally quenched. He didn't touch the food, so I nibbled on his Salisbury steak.

That night we watched the Grammys together. Howard went back to his almost-flat position, still covered in monitoring systems. I sat right next to him in a small chair. His voice was husky, but his energy level had picked up a bit.

"It's not gonna be too long until you're up there," Howard whispered.

"And you'll be my date," I said. "Obviously you'll be the first person I thank."

My phone buzzed. It was one of Howard's colleagues. He apologized for asking but needed to know what to do about the project they were working on. I relayed the message to Howard.

He pondered his answer for a moment.

"Tell him to put it on pause," he said quietly, closing his eyes.

As I texted that back, the pit in my stomach grew. This was the first time it occurred to me that Howard might feel uncertain about his future. It was unlike him to pause anything.

It had gotten late. I asked if I could sleep over, not wanting to miss a moment by my soon-to-be husband's side. Howard said I needed to go home and rest. The night nurse agreed that he was in good hands, and it was safe for me to leave. I objected, but they assured me it was alright.

In retrospect, maybe Howard was enjoying his time away from my snoring.

I Got You Babe

34
MONDAY

I put Howard's squat little upside-down bottle of toothpaste on the shelf above the bathroom sink, stacked his clothes in the closet, and emptied his backpack into yet another bedside table. We were back in the oncology wing—the scare from the ICU behind us—and would stay here until his health stabilized enough for us to go home.

My phone rang from an unknown number. I picked it up. It was someone from City Hall, sounding confused as he explained that he'd been told to call me and schedule an appointment for a marriage license as soon as possible.

"Typically, we're scheduling three to five months out," he said. "But my boss told me to prioritize you two because of your fiancé's condition." He gave me instructions for our appointment at the County Clerk's office on Thursday morning.

I thanked him and hung up the phone.

"Helps to know people," Howard whispered with a wry smile. He'd had his friend and former mayoral chief of staff Rick Jacobs make a couple of calls. I felt bad for cutting in line. But my forever guy had a valve in his neck, so I decided to accept the gift and say some prayers of gratitude.

While I was confident in the hospital staff's ability to handle Howard's medical needs, there were a couple of practical items I needed to keep his morale and comfort high.

First, I found the water station. Howard's throat was severely irritated from thrush—a side effect of his treatment in the ICU. Over the past twenty-four hours, his once-booming voice had been reduced to a scratchy whisper. He said it was painful, like the worst strep throat imaginable. Cold liquids helped, so buzzing for a nurse and waiting wasn't an option. I fetched a small brown plastic pitcher and proclaimed that we could stay in the room as long as we needed, now that we had achieved water independence.

Second, the nurses told us that Howard would need a catheter, but he didn't want to add that discomfort on top of the rest of his pain. I told them I'd handle it.

"I feel like *Human Catheter* would be an excellent name for our heavy metal duo once we get out of here," I told Howard as I held the portable plastic urinal for him. His eyes were closed, and he managed a faint smile. He did an admirable job not letting on how much he hurt, but I could tell. Especially for someone who made his career using his voice, it must've been hell to be silenced by pain.

When dinner came, he motioned for me to eat his Salisbury steak.

"Not hungry," he whispered. "You have it."

I hadn't seen him eat since I'd been there.

"I think you need something in your system," I said. I handed him his lemonade, but he took a sip and grimaced. It was mostly sugar and aggravated his sore throat. I ventured down to the cafeteria and returned with an assortment of sugar-free beverages.

Howard picked a vitaminwater flavor called *Shine*—apparently strawberry lemonade. He took a sip, and his eyes popped wide open. He smiled at me and then chugged the entire twenty-ounce bottle.

"Ahhhh!" he gasped with a giant grin on his face. "Now *this* is the most delicious thing I've ever tasted!" he whispered emphatically. His voice seemed slightly stronger.

"Okay!" I said hopefully. "I'll keep 'em coming!" I went back to the cafeteria and bought the rest of the bottles from the cooler.

I Wish I Was the Moon

35
TUESDAY

The next morning, I awoke before my alarm. Despite my persistent begging, Howard still wouldn't let me stay overnight. I'd eaten nothing but hospital food all weekend and realized I needed a long-term sustenance plan to survive until he was ready to come home.

I walked to the grocery store around the corner from Howard's house. The card reader at checkout asked for a member ID. I looked up Howard's phone number and typed it in. Then I resolved to memorize it, because Howard was going to live a long life and I needed to know it by heart. I also made a mental note to be more patient, because you never know what's going through someone's head at the self-checkout.

I visualized the way the number looked on the keypad as I walked home, on the drive to the hospital, and on the way up to Howard's room. By the time I entered, I had it down.

"Good morning, angel," Howard whispered groggily. He had been sleeping. His voice was still hoarse. I called Dr. Gary for an update and asked him about it.

"The thrush has been cleared up," Gary said. "His voice is like that because his lungs are full of fluid."

He then outlined how, as predicted, each of Howard's organs were failing, but fixing one would affect the others. His delivery was sensitive, but stern. I knew he'd been here before. But now he was talking about one of his dearest friends, and he was worried. Yesterday's relief to be out of the ICU vanished.

That morning, Howard's cousin, Rabbi David-Seth Kirshner, came to visit. Howard told him that he didn't have a good feeling. His intuition was telling him "Game Over."

I shuddered at those words. Tears welled up in my eyes. My throat felt like it had been sealed off.

Rabbi David-Seth sat on the side of Howard's bed as they prayed together. Sunlight streamed through the window to his right. I sat on the side closer to the door and silently followed along. I couldn't understand the Hebrew words, but they seemed magical. It felt like they could fix everything.

"This will be the greatest story of resilience, strength, and perseverance ever written," said David-Seth.

"It will be what it will be," Howard replied. "But I'm not giving up."

"You better not! I need you and love you. And so do way too many other people."

Howard turned his head to look at me.

"I couldn't be doing this without Mike," he said. I took his hand. "He's been amazing."

Shortly after his cousin left, Howard started coughing. It sounded like he had congestion deep in his chest. After a low and hearty cough, he motioned for a tissue. He spit into it and pulled it from his mouth to reveal a large amount of deep maroon phlegm.

We soon filled a paper bag with bloody Kleenex. It seemed like he was losing a lot of blood through his lungs. His sinuses were also backed up, and he started snorting to clear them out.

"Hold on," I said, reaching for the tissues again. But he was determined to clear his nasal passages immediately. With a loud snort, he blew a fat red snot rocket. It landed all the way on the ceiling. It was so disgusting, he laughed. A young oncologist knocked and then entered the room.

"How are we feeling?" he asked Howard.

"Well," he whispered, "my lungs must still be working." He pointed to the ceiling above the doctor's head and chuckled. The doctor didn't seem amused.

"Pain level?" he asked.

"Eight and a half," Howard answered. I was shocked. He had just been giggling over a snot rocket like a grade schooler. Turns out he was soldiering through so that I wouldn't worry about him.

My pocket buzzed—it was a text on Howard's phone from Robin Roberts, wanting to know how he was doing. I knew Howard knew famous people, but it still amazed me that someone I admired from TV was checking on him.

I told Howard, and he asked for his phone. I told him he wasn't supposed to exert himself. He reached out and whisper-exclaimed, "I have to talk to Robin Roberts!" I handed it over reluctantly. It was too adorable that he used her full name. I left the room to speak with the medical team.

In the hallway they told me about the next steps for Howard's treatment plan, insisting that our morale should be high. I just nodded as they recited various surgeries, medications, side effects, treatments for those side effects, ultimately culminating in a bone marrow transplant. "We see a clear path forward" had become their catch phrase.

When I got back into the room, Howard was off the call with Robin. He was now using his phone to play my song "Through the Changes" for a nurse.

"This is you?" she asked as she worked. Howard turned his head to look at me, smiling. I bashfully said that it was. "Wow," she replied. "Your voice is amazing!"

"That's my talented man," Howard whispered proudly.

He waved his hands back and forth ever so slightly as he listened, like an off-duty orchestra conductor. When I played a long run on piano, he mimed it with me, his hands gliding along an imaginary keyboard in the air.

Pride overtook my embarrassment. He genuinely loved my music.

He sang along with my lyrics in his gravelly whisper. I smiled at the way he was so consistently behind, as if the first word of each line was a clue to the rest of the lyric. I filed it away with my "Endearing Things About Howard" memories.

That afternoon we met with a hospital administrator, the oncology team, and Dr. Gary to put our marriage plan in place for Friday morning. We wanted to have a ceremony in one of the nice lobbies with family and friends. The medical team consented, provided Howard was healthy enough for the move, and the guests kept their distance. The administrator said she'd put a hold on the area for us, with a conference room down the hall as a backup. Worst case scenario, we would be married in Howard's hospital bed with just the officiant and a witness present.

When I was younger, I'd imagined someday getting married in front of a large audience of my family and friends. Of course, until I was in my twenties, this scenario took place in a Catholic church, and the person standing opposite me was a woman.

When I finally started living my authentic life as an adult, this vision changed. My forever guy and I would both wear black tuxedos. The officiant would be someone dear to both of us equally, and the bridal party would be a mix of male and female friends and family. My sister would be my best person. We wouldn't be in a church, but on a beach—or, since I hate sand getting everywhere, maybe a grassy park near the water. And most importantly, there would be hundreds of chairs full of our friends and family.

The recessional song would be "Signed, Sealed, Delivered," and our loved ones would sing along as we strutted down the aisle hand-in-hand, ready to party at the reception with a live band made up of my musician friends. I would sit in and sing a dedication for my new husband.

Howard and I had been discussing our wedding for months, and I liked our two tuxes and food trucks plan. I had to keep my chin up as that vision faded. We were going to be husbands, and that was the important thing.

I sat in Howard's bed as he texted the good news to his family and friends. We all needed something positive, something to look forward to. They each responded in their own way, happy for us. Howard replied that he was grateful for me, his bashert. It wasn't lost on me that Howard could still see a higher power at work while he texted from a hospital bed, having been diagnosed with the most aggressive form of leukemia just five days earlier.

He assured his family, "I'm not going anywhere."

Howard shared with me that he told his nieces and nephews he had "too much to live for." He said he needed a few more decades to watch his great-nephews grow up. I told him I needed the same.

"You promised me forty years, remember?"

Helpless
"I beg God for a bargain"

36

Howard needed to rest, and as he dozed, I went for a walk to get some air and call my parents. When I told them the wedding plans—and that I would be moving to California as soon as Howard was out of the hospital—they didn't hesitate. They congratulated me right away and said to pass it on to Howard, too.

I was relieved, but it was bittersweet. I love my parents. They'd given me every opportunity growing up and a moral compass that still steered me through adult life. We'd lived several hundred miles apart for most of it, and I always wondered what it'd be like to live closer to my family.

When I moved to Nashville in 2020, I got my answer. I was close enough for weekend visits to watch football and fire up the grill. It felt good to be around in person more often, and I wanted to be nearby to help as they aged.

When it became clear that I'd be moving to Los Angeles, I worried about living across the country from them. I was torn. But they sounded genuinely excited for us to get married, which of course meant living together. I promised them I'd visit even more than I did when I was just a few hours down I-40.

Before I returned to Howard's room, I got a call from his Aunt Manya. After I updated her on Howard's health and our wedding plans, she shared a secret with me. Howard had called her in late January, saying that he was worried about his health, and afraid of how I'd react. She told him to be honest with me, and that was when he called to offer me "an out."

It hadn't occurred to me what deliberation Howard must have gone through before that call. In our time together, I'd heard him tell all kinds of important people what they needed to do in tough situations. He was like a crisis management computer; in mere seconds, he could parse a mountain of data and compute a solution.

Picturing him wrestling with uncertainty in this most important area—us—nearly broke my heart. What was it? Surely not that he loved me so much, he'd rather see me go free than stay and care for him. Maybe he just needed to take control of the situation and lead me out the door rather than risk me running away.

That evening while Howard slept, I begged God to let him live. I'd just found my best friend, my soul mate, my forever guy. It couldn't be over already. I told God that I would trade everything I'd been working on to care for him, if I could just have a few more years.

No matter how long it took, I'd be there. I would rather stop everything I was striving to achieve than accomplish my goals alone and have to think, *I hope Howard can see me*. Without Howard, nothing would ever feel entirely joyous. No pleasure would ever be free of pain. I'd never be whole.

Howard woke up and told me to go home and get some sleep. I asked if I could stay, but he again said no.

I Live for You

WEDNESDAY

I woke up before my alarm again, not sure if I'd slept at all.

> Good morning, I love you
> Do you need me to bring anything?

> Just my man

> OK I'm on my way

I slurped some coffee and checked my phone to make sure nothing was blowing up at work before I headed out. There was a rather lengthy email from my client in San Diego—the one who had just threatened to fire me, then kept me on but said she couldn't spend any more money on the project.

I had texted her that Howard was in the hospital fighting for his life, and I wouldn't be able to work on her record until he was better.

But she didn't seem to care, as she had been reviewing the work from our most recent session and wasn't happy. She wanted me to purchase a guitar to work on her songs at his bedside. She said that her music would be healing.

I was shocked. And put off. I didn't have time for this. I quickly replied that I needed to focus on Howard, and that—as I'd already informed her—I would not be working on her album until he was back in good health.

In response, she blew up. She sent an even longer email alleging that I'd stolen ideas from her, recycled my own ideas into her work, and scheduled my releases to purposefully compete with hers.

At first, I thought it was a joke. I quickly checked her Instagram and verified that nearly half of her followers were originally friends and fans of mine—I had promoted her music far more than any producer had ever promoted me. I checked release dates and saw that the song she accused me of stealing from her was released before I'd even met her. As far as recycling the idea of blending songs into one another to form a cohesive album? I didn't invent that, so I wasn't sure where to begin.

I needed to be by Howard's side, but these accusations had me paralyzed. Pain, anger, and confusion swirled so rapidly in my head that my body trembled. Typically, I would run something like this by Howard for his opinion on how to handle it, but I wouldn't bother him with this right now. I pictured him at the hospital, alone. I needed to get there, but not in this state. There was only one way I could clear my head.

I replied, "I need to block you now."

The moment I hit the block button, I felt my neck and shoulders coming free from the tension.

We attach ourselves to people, places, and ambitions, wanting to make them work. Sometimes it's hard to discern which are worthy endeavors and which are holding us down—especially when the former evolve into the latter. The wanting remains, even when the utility has passed. We stay tethered to sunk costs. Optimists like me will sink all the way to the bottom holding that rope. But it's incredible how once we sever those restraints, we're propelled toward what we really need. My focus snapped back to Howard.

The phone rang. It was Dr. Gary.

"Howard had a really rough morning," he said. "You need to get here soon."

"Wait, what?" I said in disbelief. "I texted him; he didn't mention anything was wrong."

Dr. Gary said that Howard had been in agony all night and hadn't slept at all. They were bringing his pain level down now, but his numbers weren't good. Panic elbowed every other thought out of my mind, causing my body to constrict once again, like being stuffed into a locker by a grade school bully.

I skipped a shower and breakfast, pulling my shirt and shorts on as I rushed downstairs. Double-checking that I had my wallet, phone, and keys, I surveyed the kitchen to make sure everything was off. I prayed that I would not return to this place a widower. Howard and I would be in that kitchen together again, making dinner, pausing to slow dance and smooch to the Rat Pack. As I flipped off the lights I said aloud, "I will be back here with Howard."

L.A. traffic was kind that morning, and the trip to Cedars was a blur. I trembled as I waited in line to check in and then hustled up the elevators to the oncology department.

"Good morning, sweet angel," Howard said quietly as I stormed into his room. I had expected the worst. Although he looked a little pale, he was still my handsome Howard.

"I got the proof of hospitalization this morning," he said slowly. "What else do we need for the marriage license?"

I was being pulled in three directions from minute to minute. Howard remained calm although I knew he was in pain, the oncology team saw a "path forward," and Dr. Gary warned that the situation was far more critical than anyone was letting on.

There was a knock on the door. Howard's oncology team entered, accompanied by Dr. Gary and a new person who was introduced as David Kessler, an expert on hospice care and grief. I bristled.

As the oncology team unpacked their plan for the next steps, I sat on Howard's bed by his waist, holding his hand and taking mental notes. He had raised the head of his bed slightly to make eye contact with the doctors. When they finished detailing several surgeries to reverse the damage caused by the first round of chemo, then blasting him with more chemo once he was healthy enough for it, then nursing him back to health a second time for a blood transfusion followed by a bone marrow transplant, my head was spinning.

Howard snapped me back to reality when he simply said, "No."

My consciousness left my body from the shock. I felt dizzy. From somewhere near the ceiling I watched the oncology team mirror my confusion. One of the young doctors began to speak.

"But we see a path for…"

"I don't want that," Howard interrupted. "I've seen this before."

His tone was steady and sure despite the reduced volume. I felt his frustration at not being able to use his booming voice. But his whisper spoke louder.

Howard didn't want to endure the pain and suffering of these procedures just to acquire six more months—potentially—of time on this planet.

"I've had an incredible life," he said. "I did everything I ever wanted to do. And I got to experience true love." He squeezed my hand as he spoke. "I'm ready to go."

Apparently, the decision to invoke hospice care had been made without me in the room, because Howard, Dr. Gary, and David Kessler all seemed on the same page about it.

But I felt blindsided. How bad could last night have been? I couldn't imagine what kind of torment might have pushed him from "I have too much to live for" to "I'm ready to go" so fast. I couldn't take it.

"NO!" I shouted, releasing his hand. "You have to keep fighting."

Suddenly we were alone in a crowded room. I begged Howard to stay with me, as if we were the last two people on Earth and he had decided to blast off in a jetpack. I crawled on top of him like a giant lap dog.

"No! It's not over! You're Howard Fucking Bragman. You're fucking bulletproof! You're a fucking badass and you're not giving up." I cried. I shouted and squeaked through the tears. I was on top of him, straddling him, imploring him. He looked into my eyes calmly, lovingly, and waited patiently to let me get it all out.

"You wanted a captain, well here's your fucking pep talk, and I'm telling you you're not fucking done! You have to keep fighting. We're getting married and I fucking need you to fight for me."

I did my best not to crush him while I melted down. I put my forehead next to his. My tears rolled down his stubbly cheeks. He sighed.

"Alright," Howard said. I opened my eyes, returned abruptly to a room with a half-dozen other people. I leaned back to see his face. He rolled his eyes at me.

"Fine, angel, I'll do it."

I hugged him as best I could and kissed his lips through my mask.

He conceded to the two non-invasive tests that the team wanted: a CT scan to assess his lungs and gall bladder, and then kidney dialysis.

"Thank you," I whispered. I had a good feeling for the first time in days. This was going to work. We were going to save Howard's life.

Castles Made of Sand

The nursing staff rearranged the tubes and cables, set the portable monitors onto the extension at the foot of Howard's bed, and we began the process of maneuvering him out of the room, down the corridor, and into the elevator to go downstairs for imaging.

As we walked behind the bed, Dr. Gary leaned over to me. "Well done," he said. Then he added, "I think I counted thirteen 'fucks' in that speech." I nodded and wiped tear streaks from my face.

When we got down to the first floor for imaging, the CT machine wasn't ready for us. Howard lay flat in his bed while Dr. Gary, David Kessler, Howard's nurse, and I stood around him in the middle of a large noisy room with staff members hustling about, tending to other waiting patients.

This area was far more chaotic than oncology.

They backed Howard's bed into a holding stall, separated from the other patients by just a curtain on either side. There was far less privacy and a lot more commotion here. The minutes dragged into hours. Each time Howard needed to urinate, I asked for privacy— but we never got it. We were in the cattle call area of the hospital, with nurses and other patients milling about, and the curtain didn't wrap all the way around our stall. I sensed Howard losing his patience each time a stranger glanced our way while I held his urinal for him. It was the first time I saw Howard on the verge of losing his temper—with me or anyone else—the entire week. But he kept his composure.

"See?" he said with an emphatic eye roll. "This is what I didn't want."

As we neared our second hour of waiting, I was beginning to second-guess myself.

Then it was finally our turn. I held Howard's hand until it was time to move him into the CT machine. The process of lifting a six-foot-four bear of a man was not elegant. Again, he rolled his eyes.

"See?" he again implored me. I had to let go of his hand and wait outside in the hall.

"You'll be okay, honey," I said as I left. He didn't respond.

Waiting out in the hallway, picturing Howard alone and cold in that imaging machine, I knew that this wasn't right for him. A larger-than-life, fearless trailblazer, a titan of the LGBTQ+ community, a man with all the answers, he should be calling his own shots.

But how hard do you press someone to keep fighting for their own life? It's an impossible balance. If I said nothing and he died, I would never be able to live with myself. If I pushed too hard and prolonged his suffering, he would resent me—and eventually I would have to live knowing that we parted on bad terms.

Should I be Howard's team captain and persuade him to fight? Or should I be his cheerleader and show him my support?

A different porter came to return us to the room. I was so out of it I didn't notice we weren't taking the same route back. When the doors slid open, I saw that these were not the extra-large transport elevators we had taken down. These were the pedestrian elevators.

"Are we going to fit?" I asked.

The porter shrugged, now noticing that this bed was not standard length. "We should," he mumbled unconvincingly.

We all crammed into the elevator, and the door slid shut onto the end of Howard's bed. An alarm buzzed loudly. The porter pulled in and jerked the head of the bed diagonally, rocking Howard back and forth. David, Dr. Gary, the nurse, and I all shimmied to fit around the sides. The alarm was piercing.

"These elevators were closer," the porter mumbled as he rather violently jerked the handles on the bed, jostling Howard even more. He rolled his eyes again.

"See?!" Howard held his palms to the sky helplessly as he rocked back and forth with the porter's efforts. He began to cough uncontrollably. It looked and sounded painful. As he struggled to breathe while the porter jostled him this way and that, my heart sank deeper. I felt awful for forcing him into this.

Finally, the doors closed and the buzzing stopped. We were heading up. I breathed deeply. Then the elevator stopped. The doors opened. A woman on the other side stood dumbfounded at the sight of us all crammed into this elevator.

"I'll wait," she said.

Someone hit the "Door Close" button. I looked down at Howard and squeezed his hand. I thought, *No way we get stuck again. Please, God, do not let us get stuck again.*

When the doors closed again on Howard's bed and the alarm shrieked, everyone in the elevator collectively groaned.

"Oh great," Howard said with yet another eye roll. "Why don't you all just leave me here."

I knew he wasn't aiming this frustration at me. At least, not entirely, and not intentionally. But I felt responsible.

As the transport vigorously shook his bed back and forth to find the exact angle again, Howard and I looked at each other. He didn't look sad. Or upset. He just knew. He told me without words that he didn't need a team captain right now. He needed a cheerleader. He needed his soon-to-be husband to fully support him and accept his decision to leave his life peacefully.

I wanted to. I just wasn't there yet.

I felt horrible about the debacle, but Howard had thick skin, and he'd surely shake it off. I prayed that whatever was in that CT scan would give him hope. I prayed that tonight's dialysis would give him strength. I prayed that after our wedding, when we were husbands, he would change his mind about hospice.

Finally back in the room, Howard dozed on and off until dinner arrived. He once again pushed his Salisbury steak my way and opted for his new favorite vitaminwater. I sat on the side of his bed as I ate.

"Babe," he whispered.

"Yeah honey?"

"I'd like you to stay with me tonight."

I put down my fork and turned to face him. He looked into my eyes calmly, arms by his sides. I rested my hand on his.

"Yeah, of course."

I couldn't finish eating. I leaned across Howard's legs, my elbow on his bed, and stared at the floor. We sat in silence for a while.

"You know," Howard said. "The day we got here, I loved napping with you."

"Me too," I said.

"You loved napping with yourself?"

He loved that fucking joke. He could barely speak, but he managed to trap me in it once again. It tickled him, and he smiled, which made him cough. It was my turn for an eye roll.

"Seriously," he whispered, his eyes closing. He was drifting off to sleep. "It was one of the sweetest moments of my life."

I Think It's Going to Rain Today

39
THURSDAY

Sunlight peeked through the window next to my green leather sleeper chair. Without looking at the clock, I knew it was very early because the doctors had yet to come for their morning rounds. It felt less like waking up and more like giving in to staying awake.

I'd finally gotten my wish to remain by Howard's side through the night. I had pulled my oversized chair up against his railing in a futile attempt to mimic our normal sleeping arrangements—with Howard closest to the bathroom and me by the window air conditioning unit. I shrugged off the aches of barely sleeping and let my eyes adjust to the light slowly turning the room from gray to golden.

It occurred to me that just one week ago, I was packing to spend this entire month with Howard. His birthday presents were tucked into my suitcase. I was planning my proposal, unaware of the cancer that was wreaking havoc on his body, unaware that we'd be married much sooner than planned.

I quietly moved around the foot of his bed and into the bathroom to pee, brush my teeth, and splash some water on my face. When I emerged, Howard was still snoozing. His bare chest moved up and down slowly. Sleeping peacefully in the golden morning light, Howard looked as handsome as ever.

I burst into tears.

Not wanting to wake my fiancé, I retreated to the bathroom. The sobs came uncontrollably, and I silenced them as best I could. My chest felt ready to burst; my body heaved involuntarily. The tension built from my neck up into my forehead, and I felt tears rolling down my cheeks. I needed to procure our marriage license this morning. I needed to pull myself and the necessary documents together. I needed to be strong for Howard.

I splashed more water on my face, looked in the mirror and implored myself to stop crying.

Opening the door, I tiptoed back to my side of the bed. I quietly lowered the railing and laid next to him awkwardly, partially on the arm of my sleeper chair, not wanting to wake him. He looked peaceful, innocent, and there was nothing I could do to help him. The tears snuck up on me once again, and I buried my face into the mattress above his head.

I felt Howard stirring and wiped my cheeks on the sheet.

"Good morning I love you," I whispered to Howard when he opened his eyes.

He smiled faintly.

"Good morning, sweet angel," he replied softly. His voice was rough, like feet shuffling up a gravel driveway.

"I have to pick up our marriage license," I whispered. "But I'll be right back."

"Okay babe. I'll be right here."

"We're going to be husbands," I said.

Howard nodded. "My hero."

I grabbed the folder with our marriage license application and Howard's notarized absentee forms and darted down the hall. Time was precious; with everything we had done to get to this point, pulling favors and conjuring a mobile notary out of thin air, I couldn't blow our wedding by missing our appointment.

Google Maps said I had a forty-five-minute drive to the Van Nuys County Clerk's office, which would get me there right on time. It felt like I was watching myself get into the car, pay the parking fee, and pull onto the street. This was a surreal and high-pressure errand. I was also feeling foggy from lack of sleep.

My head throbbed and my heart pounded as my phone guided me on the circuitous route. I wondered if I'd ever get the lay of the land in L.A., where the roads intersect like a tossed handful of spaghetti.

Once in the Valley, I just had two turns to go. But traffic had stopped ahead of me. Construction delay. My lane was blocked off with cones, and there was a line of cars waiting. A flagger was holding a "STOP" sign pointing toward me. I looked ahead. No cars were coming. I glanced at the GPS frantically. My ETA now put me five minutes late. I stepped on the gas and entered the oncoming traffic lane as the flagger yelled at me to stop.

Suddenly there was a car coming straight at me. I swerved around it, narrowly missing a head-on collision. The driver of the other car leaned on his horn. I gave an "I'm sorry" shrug and kept driving.

There was no parking in front of the County Clerk's office. I circled the block, head spinning, sweating profusely, watching the clock tick past our appointment time. I'd seen Howard exercise his fixer prowess many times. This was my time to step up and make something happen, but I was failing.

Five minutes past our appointment time, I rounded the block, feeling helpless. A car pulled out of a spot directly in front of the building. I had never been one to believe that a higher power bestows upon us mundane gifts like parking spaces, or cares which team wins the Super Bowl. But I said a quick "thank you" to anyone who might be listening as I pulled into my rock star parking spot.

Our officiant, Mike Bonin, waited patiently for me out front. We introduced ourselves. I thanked him for agreeing to marry us and apologized for being late. As we waited in line, he told me how highly he regarded Howard, and that he was proud to be a part of his wedding.

When the clerk summoned us to her station and pulled up my reservation, I breathed a sigh of relief. We made it. That feeling vanished when the clerk said she hadn't seen an absentee form for a marriage license in several years.

"We haven't done one of these since before COVID," she said with exasperation from behind a thick pane of glass. She called another clerk to consult.

"Oh… yeah," the second clerk said deliberately, looking equally puzzled. "We changed that form years ago."

"What does that mean?" I asked, stifling my mounting panic.

"I just have to make sure to enter the information correctly so that the license is valid."

"Yes, please do that," I replied. I realized how bitchy it sounded and decided that explaining the situation might help.

"Oh no," she said, her tone softer. "I'm sorry to hear that."

Over the next hour, the two clerks worked on our marriage license. I tried to be present in conversation with our officiant, but in the back of my head I worried about Howard the whole time. The worst-case scenario played out in my mind—what if he slipped away while I was gone?

Finally, the clerk slid our license under the plastic shield. As I sighed with relief, she sternly told me that all signatures had to be "completely inside" the designated blocks. She emphasized those words like someone who's had to inform more than a few people that their weddings were invalid due to scribbling. *Great*, I thought, *one more thing to worry about. Add it to the pile.* Howard was infamous for his sloppy handwriting.

With our marriage license finally in hand, I thanked our officiant one more time, and then silently thanked President Obama for marriage equality as I jogged back to the car. I was anxious about getting back to the hospital. I didn't know how much time my forever guy had left, and I needed to be there for every second of it.

But I knew Howard. He'd want to look as good as possible on our wedding day, even though we'd agreed to wear sweats and T-shirts. I stopped by our house, ran upstairs, and grabbed some options.

Back in the hospital, my phone rang as I rounded the corner toward Howard's room. It was my parents. I paused at Howard's door. I could see through the window that he was awake, listening intently to Dr. Gary and a couple of people I didn't recognize. When he saw me looking in, he slowly held up a finger to say, "Just a minute." I answered my phone with one hand, gripping the folder with our marriage license tightly in the other.

My parents asked how Howard was holding up. I told them that he was in surprisingly good spirits. Then they asked about me. I admitted that my emotions were impossibly mixed.

"He asked me to be his husband and his widower at the same time," I said, watching my fiancé through the glass, eyes filling with tears. The words barely squeaked out around the lump in my throat.

"Well, you have to do it," my dad said with a sigh that echoed my pain. "You have to give that to each other. Just in case this is goodbye." My mom agreed.

I let that sink in for a moment.

I recalled coming out to my parents twelve years ago. They were shocked. It took them some time to come to grips with the fact that their son—football captain, Catholic, Notre Dame graduate, accountant-turned-rock-musician—was gay.

Not only did they quickly come around to support me, but they loved Howard. When I visited their house for my mom's birthday just three weeks earlier, they had framed several photos of us from our first Christmas together. I was so grateful that they hadn't merely accepted us; they were displaying us proudly in their home.

"But we're praying to God he makes it," my mom said, shifting focus back to the positive. "I just wish we could be there with you on your big day."

Both of my parents had tested positive for COVID earlier in the week. My sister was house-sitting at my place in Nashville and was just starting to show symptoms as well. I felt for my family. I knew how much they wanted to be here for me.

"It's alright," I told them. "You need to get healthy."

I hung up the phone just as the signal came for me to enter Howard's room. The wedding plans were locked in. Sadly, there was no need to worry about Howard's impaired immune system, since he would be in hospice after our nuptials. I took my mask off and kissed him.

It was the first time our lips touched in almost a month. His cheeks were stubbly, and I nuzzled up against his face.

"We're going to be husbands," I whispered, squeezing into his bed, hugging him from the side, slipping one arm beneath his neck. He leaned his forehead on my shoulder, and I kissed it slowly.

"My sweet angel," he said faintly, closing his eyes and smiling. He was too weak to hug me back, but he put his hand on my leg. I shifted my weight to allow slack for the IV tube attached to his hand. His breathing grew heavy. I released my embrace and sat upright on the side of the bed next to him.

"I ordered these for the wedding," he said, handing me his phone. We'd given up the charade that I was his phone custodian.

The Amazon app was open. I was looking at a recent order for Buzz and Woody action figures.

"How?" I asked, genuinely confused as to what role a couple of *Toy Story* toys could play in our wedding.

"What do you mean?"

"Like, how are they for the wedding?"

"We'll have them with us," Howard said, "because I'm your Buzz and you're my Woody."

"Ok mister."

I thought they seemed tacky, but I bit my tongue. We were about to tie the knot in a hospital bed wearing sweats and T-shirts, so I wasn't going to argue over a couple of plastic figurines.

Any Major Dude Will Tell You

40

Reaching over to the bedside table, I connected Howard's phone to his Bluetooth speaker. It was the same one that we had used in hotel rooms on each of our "honeymoons." Stevie Wonder Radio was queued up, and I hit play. We listened to several songs in silence. Howard's eyes were closed, but his fingers wiggled gently to the groove.

"Am I allowed to ask for Steely Dan?" he whispered with a smile.

"You can listen to whatever you want," I said, putting on "Any Major Dude Will Tell You."

I sensed Howard enjoying his power play—listening to his favorite band while watching me listen to my least favorite band. I was in no position to veto a song request now.

Howard's brother Alan arrived. He seemed dazed as he entered the room, unsure of what to say.

When Howard saw him, he said, "Don't be sad, Alan, I'm fine—I never have to go to the gym again in my whole life!"

Alan just shook his head but managed a smile. They spoke, although I sensed that much more was said than was in their words. Howard was Alan's younger brother by four years. I couldn't imagine what must be going through his mind, having lost his wife to cancer recently and now seeing his little brother like this.

When Alan left to get settled in at the house, Howard drifted back to sleep. Soon there was a knock on the door. It was Howard's friends Jeanne Phillips and Liz Flynt—widow of the late Larry Flynt and now head of HUSTLER.

They smiled as they entered the room, though the concern was clear in their eyes. I knew that both women had lost their husbands in recent years. Being in a hospital must have brought back terrible memories. I was grateful for their strength in showing up for their friend.

"Hey," Howard said with a smile, "who wants to go out old and decrepit? I get to go out a star!"

"Yes, you will, Howard," said Jeanne. She and Liz smiled, their friend lifting the mood like only he could. The consummate entertainer tended to his visitors from his hospital bed as if he were hosting a party at his home.

I recoiled in sadness at Howard's jokes. But I understood that these moments weren't about me and remained quiet, not allowing myself to cry. I suspected that Howard had been breaking the hospice plan to his close friends privately. Or maybe it was just understood that the presence of unmasked visitors after a week of telling everyone to stay away meant he was ready to move on.

The conversation eventually turned to the funeral. Liz and Jeanne suggested a blowout in Los Angeles with a big guest list including all the celebrities that Howard knew. But he preferred a small ceremony in Flint with just his family present.

I squeezed his hand. While they talked, I wondered how many couples had ever discussed funeral arrangements on the eve of their wedding.

"Well," Jeanne said, "why don't we follow it with a celebration of life for all of your friends in L.A.?"

"A lot of people would like to celebrate you," agreed Liz.

Howard pondered that for a moment and concluded that he'd like a memorial after the funeral.

Howard's niece Lizzy and her husband Tom arrived soon after Jeanne and Liz left. I sat with them for a while and then realized I needed something back at the house. I excused myself to call Alan.

"Can you please bring back the presents I packed for Howard?" I asked. I heard him unzipping my suitcase and starting to sift through it.

"Mike," he said, "I know we're brothers now, but I really don't want to know this much about you."

I remembered at that moment that I had packed a handful of colorful jockstraps with brand names like "Aussiebum" and "Nasty Pig," and now Alan had to move them to get to the packages. I chuckled as I apologized to my new brother-in-law.

When I got back to the room, Lizzy told me she and Tom were going to bring back a proper family meal.

Howard and I were alone once again. He lifted the head of his bed so he could sit upright.

"I've been thinking about my memorial," he said.

"You're not dying," I answered flatly, clinging to my hopes that positive CT results, dialysis, and seeing his friends and family would change his mind.

"Okay babe, but if I did, I want there to be live music."

"Alright," I sighed. "What do you want?"

"First, I'd like k.d. lang to sing her version of 'Hallelujah.' Then, Stevie Wonder should play his version of 'God Bless the Child.' And then I want you to close with your version of 'The Best.'"

"Wow," I said. "Well, first of all, you're not dying."

Howard put his hand on mine as I spoke.

"Second, how the hell do I track down k.d. lang and Stevie Wonder?" I paused. Howard smiled knowingly.

"Alright," I sighed. "But in that lineup, I definitely don't go last!"

"That's the way it's gotta be, babe," Howard said, closing his eyes definitively and lowering the head of his bed.

I sat next to him for a few moments, letting this request sink in. Howard was just trying to make it to our wedding in the morning. I wasn't going to be planning a honeymoon for us. I was going to be planning a funeral. I felt dizzy.

"How am I going to keep going without you?" I asked, leaning over to put my face in my hands. I felt so helpless, I couldn't look at him. I felt like I was letting him down.

"One day at a time," Howard said calmly. He lifted his hand to touch my leg. I looked over and could see he felt for me. Yet he was so matter-of-fact, I couldn't comprehend it.

Alan, Lizzy, and Tom came back with dinner. Alan had brought my birthday presents for Howard. Too weak to open them himself, I opened and presented them, feeling good that he liked everything I'd picked out. He once mentioned that his father had a "B'nai B'rith Bowling" shirt, and he wished he still had it. So I tracked down the logo and had one made, with his name on the chest pocket.

"You really do pay attention," Howard whispered.

Both Sides Now

41

Once the family had gone home, we waited.

And waited.

There was no way we could transport Howard to the dialysis wing in his condition, especially after the CT ordeal. After some back-and-forth, the doctors agreed to send a mobile unit to us. They said it would arrive around midnight, and that he could sleep through the procedure.

With my sleeper chair in its spot touching Howard's bed, I put my hand on his, and we tried to get some sleep until the dialysis began. But because Howard was still in critical condition, nurses checked in on him every hour. There was no chance of sleeping with constant interruptions for vital sign checks and to distribute medication.

Around 2:30 a.m., the door flew open after a half-hearted knock, and all of the lights turned on before we could register what was happening. I got the distinct impression that the dialysis tech didn't like away games. We had yet to begin, and it already was not going as smoothly as promised.

As the tech set up her machine, she noticed that Howard's mouth wasn't covered. "Put your face mask on," the tech said to Howard matter-of-factly.

Howard chuckled, whispering, "Why, you think you're going to give me an infection and kill me?"

I shook my head. The tech had no idea what was going on in this room—that she was simply giving her patient the few extra hours he needed to leave this world as husband and husband with me. My hope that this would change his mind was dwindling.

"I won't do this procedure unless you're wearing a mask," the tech said shortly. Clearly this was more about her than Howard. I helped him put a mask over his mouth while he rolled his eyes.

Once he was hooked up to the machine, I covered Howard's eyes with his sleep mask, then pulled mine over my own. Just as I felt myself drifting into sleep, a piercing beep jolted me awake. The machine began whirring—not a soothing background hum, but a mechanical, attention-grabbing series of arrhythmic noises interspersed with periodic beeps.

I lifted my mask and looked over at Howard. I couldn't see his face, but I could tell he was in discomfort; his brow was furrowed behind his eye mask.

About an hour into the procedure he asked weakly, "How much longer?"

The tech answered, "A little over two hours." I looked at the clock. It was going on 4 a.m. My heart sank. I couldn't imagine what Howard was thinking. Then he let us both know.

"Stop the machine right now."

"What?" the tech said, looking up from her work. She was genuinely confused.

"Stop it right now," Howard repeated, growing aggravated. "I didn't want this; you need to stop the machine. Right. Now."

"Howard," I said, panicking. "Your blood is in that machine. She can't just stop it."

"I don't care!" he shouted, raising his voice louder than I had heard in days. It was shocking to hear his voice booming again. I leaned over the arm of my chair to put both hands on Howard's arm, attempting to soothe him. It didn't help.

"I didn't want this! It hurts! I said no more invasive procedures!"

My heart shattered for him. And for us. My hopes of this procedure turning the momentum back in our favor were gone. I just wanted Howard to be okay.

"Can you turn it off?" I asked the tech, surprised any words could get around the lump in my throat.

She was dumbfounded. "I don't think so."

Our night nurse rushed in and assessed the situation. "I'm texting your doctor. He'll get back to me and we can see what to do."

"No! Turn this machine off immediately," Howard said. He spoke with urgency and authority. I had seen hospital patients panic before—I'd been there myself—this was not that. This was a man who was used to calling the shots. He was no stranger to stressful situations. And he had no fear as he put his foot down for the last time.

Once the blood was returned to my fiancé's body, and the room cleared, Howard was asleep within minutes. I cried. I prayed. I begged God one more time for a miracle.

Let It Be

42
FRIDAY

When I heard a cautious knock at the door, morning light was barely starting to creep in the window. My right hand was still resting on Howard's left forearm, just above his white plastic hospital bracelet. I needed every last moment our skin could touch.

Howard's eyes were still closed. His chest rose and fell slowly, and he wheezed as he caught each breath. His face was almost fully bearded. I knew he disliked it, but to me he looked ruggedly handsome.

We were getting married today. I was so proud I almost forgot where we were.

The extra-wide hospital door opened just as I groggily called out, "Come in."

It was one of the two young oncologists on the team.

"We hear you had a rough night last night," he said.

Howard opened his eyes slowly. I watched them focus on the doctor as he woke up. His brow furrowed slightly as he recalled the chaos just hours before.

"You think?" he whispered.

I knew that in his mind, he was giving his most emphatic eye-roll—the one that moved his whole head in a circular motion. But he did not have the strength for it.

"Why didn't you finish the dialysis?" the doctor asked.

Howard sighed.

I jumped in. "Because it hurt. Because you said that it would be non-invasive, but it was painful. You said he'd be able to sleep through it, but it arrived late and was so noisy. It was just horrible. He doesn't want this. He's made up his mind, and he doesn't want any more pain."

It felt like someone else's voice speaking.

"And he deserves to make that decision," I added, squeezing Howard's hand gently. "He's had an incredible life."

The doctor nodded—listening but not really hearing—then proceeded to rattle off another string of procedures, multiple surgeries attending to nearly every organ in Howard's body. His lungs were full of fluid, his gall bladder needed draining. They had to improve Howard's health so he could receive more chemotherapy, then get him stable enough for a bone marrow transplant, which could potentially add six months to his life. The doctor concluded that he didn't understand why Howard would go on hospice care after the wedding, when they could "see a path forward."

I could sense Howard bristling.

"No," he said quietly but matter-of-factly. It was a struggle for him to speak. "I'm at peace. I'm getting married today."

He turned to me as he whispered the second part, smiled, and closed his eyes. Howard Bragman. A fearless, outspoken giant of a man who lent his voice to those who'd been silenced. He now turned to me to be his voice.

The doctor started to speak, but I cut him off.

"Please leave us alone," I heard myself tell the doctor, resting my cheek on Howard's shoulder.

He hesitated but then left the room. I didn't detect disappointment so much as bewilderment. He honestly did not get it. End-of-life agency must not be covered in the med school textbooks. Or maybe he was eager to try out all the procedures, like the young doctors on *Grey's Anatomy*, thirsty to apply their newfound medical knowledge.

I eased out of my chair and into Howard's bed. There was just enough room for me to lie on my side, not putting any weight on him, and slip my right arm underneath his neck. My backside hung off the edge of the bed, but the locking wheels on the sleeper recliner held me in place and kept me from falling onto the floor. This was the only way I could stay as close as possible to Howard without smothering him. I couldn't be his lummox anymore.

The sun was still only thinking about painting our room in early-morning gold. Howard had already fallen back to sleep. I kissed his cheek. His stubble felt wonderful on my lips.

No more than a few minutes had passed when another gentle knock came at the door. Howard's eyes opened, locked with mine, and without words told me, "Can you believe this shit?"

The other young doctor on the team opened the door slowly, shrugging her way into the room with a little more courtesy than her colleague.

"Good morning," she said with an innocent smile. "And happy wedding day."

I braced myself for the bad-cop/good-cop routine they clearly had devised in the hallway.

"I just wanted to check in on you. I heard it was a rough night last night."

Yes, the word had gotten around. I wondered if anyone had ever stopped dialysis mid-procedure. From the tech's baffled reaction, I doubted it. And perhaps now Howard would become a legend for *that* in addition to everything else he'd accomplished in his remarkable life.

She opened her monologue delicately with those predictable words: "Howard, we see a path forward for you."

I could feel Howard's body tensing as he turned his head to address the doctor. I didn't let him start.

"No," I said sharply. I'd never addressed a doctor that way before. I felt like a puppy who had startled himself with his first real bark.

"We had the worst day yesterday. I convinced Howard to keep fighting because I trusted you when you said the procedure would be painless. But it was awful."

My stomach clenched; my chest tightened around shuddering breaths; my nostrils burned.

"You don't know Howard," I squeaked. "Most people would be proud to have accomplished a quarter of what he has. He lived the fuck out of his life, and he deserves to leave it on his own terms."

Even as they left my mouth, I didn't believe I was saying those words. There was no stopping the tears after realizing what I'd just done. I buried my face in Howard's blankets. He squeezed my hand.

The doctor didn't move. After a few seconds she started to speak. I cut her off.

"I'm finally coming to terms with letting him go. Last night, we reached our peace. And now you come back here, making us question that? You're making me wonder if I'm going to regret this for the rest of my life. This is torture. We're getting married today. It was going to be a happy day. Please, leave us alone."

"Okay," she said, slowly leaving the room. The door closed softly behind her, and we were once again alone.

"That's my man," Howard whispered.

Chapel of Love

43

It was still early. My heart rate settled back to normal. Howard dozed off again, and I followed.

Seemingly minutes later, my alarm went off. It was time to get up and prepare for our wedding. Howard was still asleep. I tried to ignore the venue and focus on what we were celebrating—our public declaration of love and commitment.

I quietly brushed my teeth, watching my fiancé rest from the bathroom door. Then I went to the closet and stood staring at a stack of T-shirts and sweatpants. Instead of two tuxes, we were about to be joined forever in gym clothes.

If people only got one sheet of paper upon which to draw our lives, how soon it would be a mess of scribbles and colors, a picture reimagined and redrawn into unintelligibility.

Howard began to stir. I wiped my eyes and smiled at him from across the room. "Good morning, husband."

He grinned from ear to ear. "Not yet!"

And with that, he sat up straight, swiveled on his butt, and swung his legs over the edge of the bed, sending cables and tubes flying in all directions. I panicked, rushing to his side to keep him from bolting out of bed.

"Wait, you're attached…"

He was standing up and in my arms before I could finish the sentence.

He was *Howard* again. He started pointing and directing. First, we went to the bathroom, where I helped him wash up. Then, we made it over to the closet, where he decided which T-shirts we would wear. He wasn't the least bit fazed by how casual our nuptials would be. In fact, he seemed tickled by it. We picked outfits, and I helped him shimmy into clean underwear, a blue V-neck tee, and gray sweatpants. It was a delicate dance to change while attached to monitors and IVs, but we managed, giggling with anticipation.

"We need some music," Howard said, grabbing his phone. Within seconds I heard a familiar tune coming from the Bluetooth speaker.

Going to the chapel and we're gonna get married!

He looked up from his phone, grinning. My eyes welled with tears. We kissed.

Howard leaned on me as we shuffled to the bathroom for one last look in the mirror. We laughed at each other's disheveled appearance as we tried in vain to get our hair to look acceptable.

"No showers on our wedding day, honey," I wrinkled my nose. We hadn't bathed in days, and it was obvious.

"Aw, babe," he said. "We're just two scruffy Midwestern boys, aren't we?"

He grabbed the squat bottle of toothpaste from the glass shelf. He squeezed, but nothing came out. I took it from him, turned it upside-down, and shook it.

"Babe," he said with maybe a little more than mock exasperation, "it's made so you can stand it on its cap."

"Then they really should've put the label on upside down," I said as I shook the bottle and then pasted his brush.

Back in bed, now configured to sit upright, Howard surveyed our wedding venue. He breathed heavily but had the most energy I'd seen all week. Planning an event was his wheelhouse. It thrilled me to see him alert and energized, even if his breathing was labored, his voice hushed, and he was still connected to hospital equipment.

As if reading my mind, a nurse entered and began to remove the main line from his neck. While she delicately peeled back the tape and gauze that had held it in place, Howard described where everyone should stand. He winced in pain as she extracted the enormous valve from his body.

It must have felt better not to have that giant intrusion in his neck. But it was another reminder that this wedding was to be followed by a funeral—we just didn't know when.

"Perfect," Howard chuckled. "I won't look like Frankenstein for our wedding photos."

I envisioned the hundreds of people I'd witnessed taking photos over the course of my many wedding band gigs. Bride and bridesmaids to one side, groom and groomsmen to the other, all smiling and perfectly posed from tallest to shortest. I mentally Photoshopped them into our hospital room. It didn't compute. People don't often take pictures in hospitals; we don't need to memorialize what happens there.

Our guests began to arrive.

Dr. Gary brought the Buzz and Woody plastic action figures Howard had ordered. I rolled my eyes as I dutifully perched them on the bed behind us. Buzz for Howard—the big dreamer, the action-taker, the thrill-seeker—and Woody for me—the pragmatic worrier and loyal companion.

Lizzy and Tom arrived with the floral arrangements. They had purchased real flowers and were parking at the hospital when I was told that we needed artificial ones for the oncology wing. Somehow, they procured a nice-enough-looking fake centerpiece, which Howard instructed to be placed at the foot of his bed. At my mom's suggestion, they also found two artificial boutonnieres. I pinned his flower to his V-neck T-shirt. I started to do my own but couldn't, and Lizzy came to my rescue.

Howard's brother Alan and friend Rick, who had arranged our marriage certificate meeting, stood on either side of us. The room buzzed with tempered excitement—it was crowded, with the hospital waiving our two-visitor limit for the special occasion.

I squeezed Howard's hand. He had grown quiet, his burst of energy winding down, his voice too weak to speak up. With his eyes he told me that if he had his way, he'd be the loudest, most animated one in the room. He smiled. I leaned in and kissed him.

Howard and I sat side-by-side in his bed holding hands. Lizzy knelt on his other side, holding his other hand. We all looked up at Mike Bonin as he started the ceremony.

He started by asking everyone to hold up their hands and send us their love and strength. I silently wondered if there was any amount of either that could fix this situation. Mr. Bonin continued, saying the contract of marriage is not to be taken lightly; it comes with obligations and responsibilities.

My mind instantly flashed forward to a future Howard and I once discussed, in which we moved the primary bedroom to the first floor so that an elderly Howard wouldn't have to climb the stairs. I'd already promised to take care of him for the rest of our lives. I snapped back to the present, painfully aware that I'd never get that chance, just in time to hear Mr. Bonin ask me to read my vows.

When we first planned this wedding earlier in the week, Howard and I had agreed not to exchange vows. We were to complete the minimum requirements necessary to be legally married, then Howard would beat cancer, and then we would plan a more traditional ceremony and reception. Up until very recently, I believed in that plan.

But the previous night, after the dialysis went so badly, I couldn't sleep. I knew there would be no later ceremony. This was going to be my one chance to say something.

I pulled up the words I'd written on my phone and started with, "Howard Benjamin Bragman," but my next breath caught in my throat. The words had lost their focus on the screen. I pressed on: "You are my best friend, and my guiding light." My voice cracked. Dr. Gary put a comforting hand on my shoulder. Out of the corner of my eye, I saw Howard turn his head slowly toward me.

"When the world is cold, you provide warmth. When I'm lost, you direct me. When I'm anxious, you calm me. When I feel alone, you comfort me, you understand me, and you love me."

I swiveled to face Howard.

"Our year of adventures has been the best year of my life. You are an astonishingly great man, I'm blessed to be by your side, and to have found true love. Thank you for making me the luckiest man alive."

Howard smiled and squeezed my knee. I kissed him on the cheek, and he looked up to his friend Rick.

It turned out that Howard had reached the same conclusion and had asked Rick to say something on his behalf.

"Howard told me one year ago that he's had a great life." He smiled down at his friend of over thirty years, seated before him on a hospital bed, and added, "Which he has." He drew a deep breath before continuing.

"But he said the one thing missing was true love." His voice wavered. "And he found that." Howard turned from Rick to me and smiled faintly. He was running on fumes, but I could feel his love radiating.

"You found each other," Rick continued. "There's nothing better than that. And sharing every memory that you've built and keep building is more than most people ever get—especially the love you both have." He motioned to us both as he finished, tracing our invisible bond in the air.

"Howard," said Mr. Bonin. "Do you take Michael to be your lawfully wedded spouse?"

Howard nodded affirmatively and said softly, "I do." Although he spoke quietly, I heard those two words loud and clear.

"Michael," continued Mr. Bonin. "Do you take Howard to be your lawfully wedded spouse?"

I turned my head to see Howard. He was smiling at me. With a big grin I said, "I do."

This was really happening. My senses tingled.

Mr. Bonin instructed us to join hands. Lizzy let go of Howard's right hand so that I could hold both. The officiant turned to Howard.

"Repeat after me…"

Howard took a breath and summoned the effort to repeat his line, "I Howard, take thee Michael, to be my lawfully wedded spouse." I followed suit.

Mr. Bonin concluded, "By virtue of the authority vested in me as Deputy Commissioner of Civil Marriages, I now pronounce you husband and husband, married under the laws of the State of California."

Howard leaned forward and we kissed on the lips as the room filled with applause. Howard was beaming.

Husband.

I liked that word.

"We're husbands," I whispered in Howard's ear with a broad smile. It felt magical to speak those words.

I allowed myself to celebrate in place. We didn't strut down the aisle, there were no champagne toasts, and nobody was dancing. But we were happy. Newlyweds in a hospital bed. We had overcome so much to get to this moment. It felt right to bask in it for as long as possible.

When all the congratulations had been said, and the wedding party had retired to the hallway, we had one more item of business: signing the marriage certificate.

The officiant, our witness, and I all found our boxes and signed. By now, Howard was spent, his surge of energy from the morning long dispersed. He could barely hold a pen. Sitting next to him in bed, my hand steadied his shaking wrist, imploring him to stay inside the lines. I recalled the clerk's warning and was terrified that a technicality would nullify our incredible accomplishment.

When we finished, I handed the document to Mr. Bonin and thanked him again. Turning back to Howard at my side, I leaned in to give him a kiss, but he had already fallen asleep. I kissed his cheek instead. I nuzzled the side of his face with my own. He didn't lean in and smile, or say something adorable, like he usually would. I slumped down so I could rest my head on his shoulder, staring at the hospital bed stretched out before us in a daze.

The glow was already fading. This was not how I had imagined my wedding celebration.

When I was down about where I should be in my career, Howard always told me, "Remove the word 'should' from your vocabulary." This concept came from the book he sent me after we first met, *A Guide to Rational Living*. "Nothing *should* be anything; it's just the way it is and all you can control is your response."

Well fuck that. Our wedding should've been a celebration. We should've been dancing together as husbands. We should've been partying with our loved ones, not lying in a hospital bed.

How many weddings had I played in the previous year? At every single one I had called Howard on my breaks, filling him in on any interesting details of the décor, the outfits, the venue, choreographed bridal party entrances, awkward best man toasts, bouquet and garter tosses gone wrong, drunk uncles dancing shirtless, playing "How Sweet It Is" for the cutting of the cake. We would get none of it.

I heard a knock on the door. Howard's eyes opened slightly and he smiled as Lizzy and Tom came back into the room. Lizzy presented me with a venti coffee and a small paper bag.

"What's this?" I asked.

Lizzy smiled. "You guys need wedding cake."

I reached into the bag and pulled out two Starbucks cake pops.

"Oh my god!" I gasped. "Thank you!"

I swiveled on Howard's bedside and held them up for him to see. He grinned and picked the one he wanted. He took a bite. It made us both so happy. I hadn't seen him eat solid food in nearly a week.

"Thank you, Lizzy," he said softly as he chewed. I finished mine in one big bite, smiling. At least we got our wedding cake.

Hallelujah

44

Just a few minutes later, the hospice staff introduced themselves. I sat on the bed beside Howard and watched as a nurse swapped out his oncology wristband and officially admitted Howard to palliative care. I noticed that the date of hospice admission was our wedding day and wished I hadn't watched.

The hospice doctor introduced herself. Then she looked at Howard matter-of-factly and asked, "How are you doing? What are you thinking about?"

I thought that was a stupid question. But there was an understanding in the look that they shared.

Howard replied, "I'm grateful. I'm truly grateful."

Despite his labored voice, he sounded certain. Dignified. "I'm grateful for my life, I have no regrets." He paused briefly, then decided to leave it there, nodding his head affirmatively.

The hospice doctor remarked that she had never heard someone express gratitude when she introduced herself. She elaborated, "There is a Buddhist teaching that says, if you can express gratitude at the end, you've lived a great life."

"I have," Howard said.

"And I got to experience true love." He looked at me and smiled. I was sitting on the edge of his bed next to his legs and squeezed his knee gently.

"Isn't he handsome?" Howard said, turning back to the doctor.

"He sure is," she agreed.

"You guys." I blushed. "I can hear you."

When the doctor left, Howard's family and friends followed to get lunch. I stayed with Howard. We had the room to ourselves for the first time since we awoke on our wedding day. The early afternoon sun shone brightly through the window, heating the room. I swiveled the blinds to give us some shade. Howard snoozed quietly, lying almost flat, with his covers off to the side. I took up my position on the bed next to him, rear end hanging over the edge, held in place by the back of the sleeper chair with its wheels locked.

I scrolled through Howard's music library and played a few songs. I listened in silence, watching my new husband's chest slowly move up and down, praying I'd remember how he looked, how he felt, how he smelled—praying to never forget anything about him—knowing I inevitably would.

Howard awoke and motioned for his phone. I handed it to him. He tapped the screen a few times, then laid it face down and closed his eyes.

Sparse piano chords filled the room. I felt tears coming—this was Howard's favorite rendition of "Hallelujah," Leonard Cohen's powerful hymn. I moved fully onto the bed, resting my forehead against his. He was calm. He was so calm I could barely stand it.

How could such beauty and such pain coexist? As k.d. lang breezed elegantly through two refrains, I mentally waged war against the heavens. I wanted to kick and scream and force God to let me keep my husband.

The third verse began:

> *Baby I've been here before*
> *I've seen this room and I've walked the floor*
> *I used to live alone before I knew ya*

I buried my head in Howard's shoulder. How desperately I wanted him to live, so we could live together. I didn't want to keep living alone.

> *But I've seen your flag on the Marble Arch*
> *Our love is not a victory march*
> *It's a cold and it's a broken hallelujah*

As the verse reached its crescendo, I felt something I hadn't felt in days and would never feel again.

Howard hugged me.

He wrapped his arms around me and squeezed.

Tightly.

Howard summoned the strength for one last hug. It felt like an embrace between heaven and earth. I tucked my arms underneath him and hugged him back. Tears streamed down my face and onto his.

Our squeeze subsided, and we stayed cheek to cheek, arms around each other, until the song finished.

I pulled back to look into his eyes.

"If you can't write a song now," he mused softly, "it ain't my fault, babe."

I blinked, drawing a quivering breath and trying to figure out what he meant. He cracked a faint smile. Shaking my head, I wiped away my tears and exhaled.

My heart was being demolished—and here was the wrecking ball, telling me to use it. Channel the pain into art. Howard was so cool and composed. It felt like when he told me I might or might not "make it." He wasn't going to lie and promise I'd succeed, but he believed in me. And he knew I faced a nearly impossible journey— one I'd have to take alone. I broke into uncontrollable sobs, feeling the infinite weight of his eventual absence.

That evening was finally quiet in our room. Nobody interrupted. But the silence felt heavy. No longer was there a need for hourly checking of vital signs. No more sitting up straight in bed to administer meds. I finally had my husband to myself. We were newlyweds. And we were waiting for Howard to die.

After dinner, I joined him in his bed. He smiled at me, and I kissed him. We flipped on the TV for the first time all week. He turned to AMC. There was an episode of *Dick Tracy*. We didn't say much. My new husband was content, and that was all I needed.

I couldn't leave his side. I rotated positions between holding him and lying next to him. It was a squeeze, but I wouldn't leave until he absolutely needed his space.

That time, unfortunately, did come. After *Dick Tracy*, AMC showed a series of short noir films. Howard dozed in and out while I stared vacantly at the scenes unfolding on screen. Eventually I heard him say, "Babe…"

"Yeah, honey?"

"I love you, but can you get in your chair?"

"Sure, mister," I whispered. "Good night I love you."

"Good night, sweet angel."

I pulled the recliner back into position. Now he could lie comfortably while I rested my hand on his arm.

We both slept soundly for our one night as husbands.

Waiting in the Light
"I'm not going anywhere"

45
SATURDAY

The sun crept under the bottom of my sleep mask, and the leather of my sleeper chair stuck uncomfortably to my bare back. Wiping the sleep from my eyes, I realized that it was late morning. The sun was shining through our window and heating up the room.

We had slept in. Not because we'd spent our wedding night partying with our friends and families. We just hadn't been disturbed by the usual early-morning doctor's rounds. No nurses came around to measure Howard's vital signs or administer meds. I sighed.

Howard, sleeping completely flat, began to stir. He slowly opened his eyes, looking straight up at the ceiling. From my sleeper chair I reached across his bed rail, resting my hand on his forearm.

"Good morning, husband," I whispered.

Howard gradually turned his head to look at me. He smiled with his eyes as they focused.

"My husband," he whispered.

I smiled back, although those words tore my heart in half. I couldn't have been prouder to hear them. But they fell so softly. Yesterday he had gotten what he needed. Today he sounded ready to say goodbye.

I lowered the railing between us, rotated my recliner, and crawled into Howard's bed. I wanted nothing more than to jump on top of him, be his lummox, squeeze him and smother him with kisses all day. But instead, I assumed my position hanging off the edge, resting my rear end against the back of my sleeper chair so I could hold my new husband without putting any weight on him. I kissed his lips softly.

"You know," he whispered. I waited.

"I want you to find love again."

"Howard!" I objected. I didn't want to hear it. "Shut up. We're not..."

"I mean it," he interrupted. "I want you to find love again."

His eyes were fixed on mine. I could barely stand holding his gaze. I wouldn't allow myself to think about a future without Howard. How could he possibly think this was appropriate when we'd only been married for one day?

"Just do me a favor," he said.

"What?" I asked with a sigh.

"Give me a couple weeks."

He chuckled, then started coughing. I reached for the tissues, not laughing.

"You're unbelievable," I muttered.

I curled up to his side. There were no more monitor wires to avoid—just a single tube delivering pain medication.

We stayed there in silence for a bit. I mentally flipped back through the most incredible year of my life. It wasn't the big trips, fancy meals, or hanging out with celebrities that stood out. It was the feeling that anything we did together was important—from walking the dogs to buying groceries to watching TV on the couch, it all felt like an adventure worth memorializing. I realized I'd never again do simple things like riding in the car with Howard. Never feel him caress my arm while navigating the hills. I broke down again.

"I don't know how I'm gonna do this without you," I said between sobs, wishing I could be even a fraction as composed as he was.

"Aw, babe," he said slowly. "You got this."

Despite his weakness, he spoke with authority.

"And babe?" he whispered.

"Yeah honey?" I answered, still crying.

"You better look out…" I looked around his bed, thinking I was lying on his IV tube. But a faint smile came to Howard's lips. "Because I'm gonna fuck with you."

I shook my head and wiped my tears.

"You mean like *Interstellar*?" I scoffed, rolling my eyes. "You're gonna drop some books off a shelf?"

"You'll see," he said cryptically.

He closed his eyes and was back to sleep within moments. He seemed content. I hoped he was right.

Later that morning, Dr. Gary, Alan, Lizzy, Tom, and our friend Dave joined us, bringing coffee and a breakfast burrito for me. With nothing to do but wait, we listened to Stevie Wonder Radio as we talked and Howard rested.

"What's going to happen to the house?" Howard's brother asked me. He sat in a chair at the foot of Howard's bed. I sat beside Howard, my hand on his thigh. His chest moved up and down slowly. He was asleep.

"I don't know," I answered, dropping my head into my hands. The sadness of living in Howard's house without him overwhelmed me. The anxiety of paying a mortgage and California-sized bills was crippling.

"Howard wants me to move in, but there's no way I can afford to live in L.A. by myself."

"Yeah," Alan sighed. "The cost of living out here is insane."

The rest of the room—all Los Angeles residents—concurred with solemn nods.

"You could always rent it out," Alan offered.

"Yeah," I agreed. "That might be a good idea."

"Don't rent it out," Howard suddenly spoke up, making me jump. "You're living in the house."

I turned to Howard. His eyes were only partially open.

"I'm just afraid that I won't be able to make ends meet," I said softly.

"You'll figure it out," Howard whispered, drifting back to sleep.

I looked back to Alan, who shrugged.

"Sounds like you're moving to California," he said.

"Turns out I am," I sighed.

When Howard awoke, he spoke with his nephews over FaceTime. "I'm not going anywhere," he assured them.

He was a crisis management publicist, steadfast while managing his own final crisis. Howard was nearing the end of his life, but his enormous heart and sheer willpower led him to spend the last of his earthly currency comforting his loved ones.

Slip Slidin' Away

46

In the early afternoon, once he'd assured us all that he'd be looking after us, Howard closed his eyes. By the time golden hour brought its amber glow to our little room, Howard's breathing had slowed to a crawl. When darkness fell, his breaths came at longer and more unpredictable intervals.

I lay with my right arm under Howard's neck, nuzzled beside him, my left arm across his chest—vowing to spend whatever time we had left as close as possible. Howard's family sat in chairs around his bed.

The hospice doctor checked on us.

"He can still hear you," she said. "But he's getting close."

"I love you so much, Howard," I whispered into his ear, dripping tears once again onto his pillow. "You've had the most incredible life, and I'm so grateful I got to be a part of it."

He didn't respond. His eyes were closed, mouth open. My spirit sank as I realized he suddenly looked like the people I had seen in the ICU a few days earlier. But I was certain he could hear me.

"You're surrounded by people who love you, and there are so many more out there, mister."

Texts had been coming in steadily on both our phones from family and friends, asking me to pass along messages to Howard. They all said something similar—that he'd changed their lives for the better, and that they didn't know what they'd do without him to call for guidance. It all sounded very familiar. The number of people who felt just like me was overwhelming. I read as many as I could.

Dr. Jennifer Ashton texted:

> Ask Howard to send me butterflies 🦋

I recalled the butterfly story Howard had told me of his mother's passing and the photo on his desk. I wondered if Dr. Ashton knew that story.

I put down our phones and wrapped both arms around Howard. His breathing was sporadic, coming in short, shallow waves, further and further apart.

"You're simply the best," I whispered into his ear. "Better than all the rest."

I sang to him softly, watching his chest go up and down at random. I found myself holding my own breath as I waited for his next one.

"As long as I'm here in your arms, I could be in no better place…"

When I finished, I glanced down and could see that everyone had drawn close. Lizzy held Howard's hand; Dr. Gary felt for a pulse; Alan, Tom, and Dave sat by Howard's feet.

"We love you so much," I whispered. I repeated it over and over. Every variation I could think of to let him know how loved he was, how remarkable he was, how I admired him for the extraordinary life he lived.

I knew that he knew. But it felt like what I'd want to hear as I departed. That I did good. That I gave more than I took. To be reassured that my life meant something.

There was fluid building in his throat, making a gurgling sound. The hospice doctor asked me if I wanted to clear his airway, handing me a suction tube.

I looked at her as if she were handing me a match, lit end first.

"No please," I responded, turning away, burying my face in Howard's pillow, wincing as she drained the fluid gathering in his mouth. They call the noise of breathing through this fluid the death rattle. I knew that I'd never forget that sound until it was my turn to make it.

I needed something else in my head. Softly, I sang Howard's favorite song of mine, "Through the Changes." He had proudly shown it to each one of his friends that we met, and many members of his hospital team. I wanted to sing it for him one last time. It was difficult to get through the chorus:

> *Stay with me baby*
> *Keep me safe through the changes*
> *Honestly, no sages could've seen*
> *You dancing with me*

I kissed him on the cheek when I finished singing.

He took a short breath.

The room melted away. No machines, wires, tubes—no other people in the whole world. It was just me and Howard. I felt the stubble on his cheeks as I whispered to him, inhaling as much of his scent as I could, wishing I could bottle it to revisit for the rest of my life.

From the edge of my consciousness, a familiar voice crept in.

"Slip slidin' away," sang Paul Simon. "Slip slidin' away…"

After a long pause, Howard took another short breath. It was more like a gasp. The fluid was gathering in the back of his throat again. I whispered that I loved him, and it was okay for him to go.

> *You know the nearer your destination,*
> *The more you're slip slidin' away.*

An even longer pause.

An even shorter breath.

I squeezed him around his shoulders and kissed his temple. Through my tears, I thanked him for loving me and told him that I'd miss him for the rest of my life.

> *God only knows*
> *God makes his plan*
> *The information's unavailable*
> *To the mortal man*

I waited for another breath.
I thought I might have heard one.

> *You know the nearer your destination,*
> *The more you're slip slidin' away.*

I kept waiting for another breath to come.
But it never did.
My best friend.
My husband.
My Howard was gone.

So Hard to Let Go

"Your love was so easy, it's so hard to let go"

47

I had to let go of Howard. I kissed him on the forehead, knowing it would be the last time I would feel his skin on my lips.

I moved through his hospital room in a daze, putting his belongings back into his backpack, the one he'd slung over his shoulder as we traversed the country, the one that he'd carried into the hospital, the one he figured he'd have as he walked out of this place, back into his life. Back into our life.

But I had to leave the hospital without Howard.

Alan drove us back to Howard's house. The GPS took us down Hollywood Boulevard at 9 p.m. on a Saturday night.

As we stuttered through gridlock in shocked silence, I watched a movie scene unfolding on the crowded sidewalks. A cast of actors completely unaware of my presence. Completely unaware of Howard's absence. Their lines and choreography must've been filmed at another place and time, because they weren't crying. They were laughing. They were singing. They were listening to music. They were dancing. How could anyone dance at a time like this?

Opening the door to an empty house felt like a mistake. Like there must be some other door to some other house that I was supposed to have opened.

There must be a reality somewhere in which Howard is alive. A reality in which his friends and family would still happily hear from him in the early hours, and feel the comfort of knowing he's out there, ready to fix any jam they might find themselves caught up in.

If I were lucky, there'd be a version of me that inhabits that universe—one where I didn't have to enter a house alone, didn't have to slip into an empty bed, didn't have to drift into a moment as a one when in the previous moment I was part of a two. I don't know whether that reality is the dream, or if my reality is the dream. But both cannot be reality, I'm certain.

Under the covers by myself, I felt entirely alone. I clutched my framed photo of the two of us singing "Moon River" for what felt like hours, until I eventually, mercifully, passed out.

I woke up crying before I opened my eyes. An empty feeling arrested me, would not let me out of bed. I wanted to be anywhere but in that prison.

I listened to the second-hand tick, marking time that made no sense. In no moment would I find Howard's bright smile, engulfing bear hug, or comforting voice. I drifted from one minute to the next, feeling like each one was wrong. Like there must be other minutes where Howard still existed, where we were newlyweds, but I wasn't a widower.

If I could just find a way back to the correct time, I would shuffle down the stairs and see him sipping his coffee on his office couch. After dinner we'd cuddle until he said his lummox needed to give him some breathing room. And we'd finish the day back in this bed, together.

The minutes piled up into hours and I still couldn't pull myself out of bed. What a cruel thing, time. It speeds by when you want to savor a moment. It grinds to a halt when you want to escape one.

I finally emerged to the sound of voices downstairs. Howard's relatives and friends had come over. They introduced me to the Jewish tradition of Shiva—his loved ones brought over food and filled the house with memories of my late husband.

This is significant for two reasons.

One is that with less than a year together, there was still much for me to learn about my new husband. Howard was the sun at the center of a massive orbit, and although I was proud to be the closest planet to his star, I was also the newest. Their stories filled in details of the man I loved.

But more meaningful was the fact that they showed up at all.

Howard and I had just been married the day before his death, and I was not Jewish. Yet they accepted me as his husband, saying they were grateful for my presence in his life—that he'd never seemed happier.

I knew that my comforters needed comfort, too. Grief is a revolving door, and we traded tears from one moment to the next. It felt absurd coming from "the new guy," but I told his family and friends how much he loved them. How much he spoke about them and how eager he was for me to meet them. I couldn't possibly impart anything that they didn't already know. But I figured they needed to hear it. Their hearts were broken—in a different way, but broken nonetheless. Grieving Howard together bonded us.

That evening after everyone had left, I sat alone on the couch. My phone rang. I didn't recognize the number, so I checked Howard's phone.

Ever since I'd given out my number on his CaringBridge site, I'd started cross-referencing unknown callers this way. I had been warned not to give out information to anyone. At first, I thought that this was overprotective. But by the time I'd gotten home after Howard passed, someone had posted the news on Facebook—which had been reposted and turned into a makeshift obituary, full of misinformation and speculation about the end of Howard's life.

It also referred to me as his boyfriend, not his husband.

I was dumbfounded. I knew Howard was remarkable. But this intrusion of our privacy was my first clue that my late husband was a newsworthy person—and that his notoriety would now impact my life.

I looked up the unknown number in Howard's phone. It was a woman's name, and beneath it read "Stevie Wonder Manager."

I dropped Howard's phone. Mine had stopped ringing, and frantically I pulled up my call history to tap the most recent entry and call it back.

"Hi Mike," a woman's voice said. "Please hold for Stevie."

My heart pounded.

"Michael," said a familiar voice. "Michael, I am so sorry for your loss."

"Th… thank you," I stammered. It was Stevie Wonder. I didn't know what to call him. Stevie seemed too informal. Mr. Wonder?

"We are here in this space for just a little bit," he said, "as we're assigned to our next journey."

I couldn't speak. His voice was so familiar. I'd heard it thousands of times before. But now he was talking to me. About Howard.

"Howard is a beautiful soul," he continued. "The almighty has him now. And he will unite us again in time."

I thanked him for his kindness. We said goodbye, and then I put my phone down. I grabbed a pen and scribbled his words in my notebook. I stared at it, awestruck. It felt like an angel had just delivered a message from God over the phone.

"Thank you, Howard," I said aloud.

Living Without You

48

The next morning I again struggled to open my eyes, crying and clutching a pillow to my chest before I was fully conscious. But I was pulled out of bed by familiar voices in the kitchen.

I collapsed onto the bottom step at the sight of Howard's empty office couch. No coffee mug on the table. No TV news blaring.

"Good morning, Michael," said Dr. Gary. I stood up and accepted a hug.

Family and friends sat at the kitchen table, huddled around a laptop. The task of the morning was an unenviable one—writing a press release for one of the best publicists who ever lived.

The story had already been picked up by TMZ and a few other outlets. It shocked me how fast the news had traveled, and how many people were sharing it with glowing praise for Howard. I was sad and proud at the same time. Howard would've loved the attention.

I didn't tell anyone that I hated the reports calling me Howard's "boyfriend." This wasn't about me. But I wanted the world to know that we were husbands.

Howard's nephews joined the conversation from their home in Atlanta. Adam, who had worked for his uncle at his company 15

Minutes, had composed a rough draft in anticipation of the meeting. As we collectively fleshed it out, I noticed that everyone's eyes were red. We'd all been crying for a long time.

We all jumped an inch out of our chairs as Howard's phone dinged loudly. I picked it up from the kitchen counter. Everyone recalled how often he was on his phone. It was practically part of his body.

"But you know," Dr. Gary reminded me, "we didn't hear from him as much once you came into the picture."

As I went to turn the ringer down, I saw the notification.

"Oh my God," I said. "Oprah just texted."

I had alerted her about the CaringBridge from Howard's phone. Now she offered her condolences. One passage stood out:

> The love you shared in the dense flesh will abide with you in Spirit in ways yet to unfold. Stay open to receive it. Love doesn't die; it just transforms.

It felt like another angel had just delivered a divine message. I didn't yet comprehend what it meant to "stay open," but I knew something important had just happened—Howard was changing my life yet again.

The next day I headed to the airport by myself. My parents asked if I'd be alright traveling alone. I wasn't sure, but there was no other option. Howard had wanted his funeral to be a small family gathering in Flint, and I was the only one going from L.A.

I lined up for boarding, feeling as alone in the world as I ever had.

"Mike Maimone?" asked a voice behind me. I was in such a fog that it barely registered as my name. I turned to see who it was and found the smiling faces of two old friends.

"Holy shit," I said, shocked. It was Sean Van Vleet and Mike Robinson. Our bands had played together often back in Chicago, but we'd lost touch when they moved to L.A. over a decade ago.

"Get ready for a really weird flight," I warned them as we hugged hello. Thanks to Southwest's open seating policy, we grabbed a row together. They listened as I brought them up to date on the past year of my life, breaking down several times.

"Howard sounds like an incredible guy," said Mike after I finished. "And he was pretty lucky to have you, too," added Sean.

"Thank you," I said. I was embarrassed to cry in front of friends I hadn't seen in so long. But they didn't hesitate to offer sympathy.

"So what are you guys up to?" I asked.

"Heading to start a tour," said Sean. "What's crazy is that this morning our flights were changed, and we got put on this one at the last minute."

"You're kidding," I said.

"For real," said Mike. "We weren't even supposed to be at this airport."

I silently thanked Howard for the company. Was this the transformed love that Oprah advised me to stay open to receive?

We said our goodbyes and headed opposite ways to catch our connections. I got a text as I headed to find coffee.

"Just published this story about the big guy," messaged an unknown number. I clicked on the link. It was an article by JD Heyman. I recognized his name from Howard. He was a writer and editor of the pop-culture website *Culture Wag*.

I stopped walking to read. In the article he talked about meeting Howard through his friend Chely Wright, a country music star whom Howard had helped come out.

My phone buzzed in my hand.

It was Chely Wright, offering her condolences.

Unbelievable, I thought as we exchanged texts.

I went back to the article. JD's words brought tears of pride:

> "He approached life, love, and public relations with irrepressible joy. It's wrenching to write that I'll never hear his booming voice again. I'm not alone in grief. Howard worked in show business for four decades and collected legions of admirers."

My man was beloved. JD detailed the myriad ways that Howard was a champion for people who were misunderstood. He was a hero! How had I not comprehended all of this when he was alive? I longed to tell him how proud I was to be his husband, even more now than I had already been. And that I was embarrassed for initially wondering whether associating with him might be a bad thing.

He probably would've just shrugged and said, "See?"

I sat down with my coffee. A woman wearing a Michigan sweatshirt sat across from me. I'm not one to talk to strangers, but this string of synchronicities compelled me to open my mouth.

"Did you go there?" I asked, nodding to the large maize M on her navy-blue sweatshirt.

She glanced down, double-checking what she was wearing. "No," she replied. "I just like the shirt."

I could practically feel a comforting pat on the shoulder from Howard. What had made my friends not only switch flights but switch airports? What had made JD Heyman send me his article, and Chely Wright text me the moment I read her name in it? What had made this random lady decide to wear her University of Michigan sweatshirt that day?

I wasn't alone after all. Howard was all around me, sending me signs.

Over the Rainbow

49

There was one hotel located between the cemetery in Flint and Howard's uncle's house—the one I'd driven to in the middle of the night to get Howard after his aunt's funeral.

I wondered how many of our steps I would have to retrace alone.

I had booked three rooms for my family, who were driving to meet me. I wanted to be strong for my parents. I knew that they were genetically obligated to share my pain, so I tried my best to temper it. But I couldn't. As soon as I saw them, I broke down.

"I'm so sorry," my mom said as she hugged me.

"And congratulations on your wedding, too," my dad added sorrowfully. I had inherited his propensity to look for positives in any situation. "You guys were lucky to have each other."

They had driven up from North Carolina to be with me at the funeral. My sister had been watching our place in Nashville, and she drove up with my suit. I hopped in her car to go to the cemetery. She knew Howard the best out of my family and friends, and it felt comforting to finally have someone from my life to cry with me.

I sat next to her for the service and listened to eulogies from Howard's cousin the rabbi, his brother Alan, and his nephews David and Adam. They each gave moving testaments to the ways that Howard had positively impacted their personal lives and the world in general.

Then it was my turn. Rabbi David-Seth gave me a warm introduction. I knew it would be difficult to speak, but I didn't realize how difficult. It felt like a piece of my heart was being ripped out with each word. I paused to compose myself whenever my voice crumpled and squeaked. And then, disjointed from the present, I watched myself and everyone else follow as Howard's coffin was carried out of the chapel, across the grass, and lowered into the ground.

My family and I stood silent and listened to Howard's family recite the Mourner's Kaddish. Everyone knew it from memory. The Hebrew words were unfamiliar to me. The collective incantation was mesmerizing, beautiful, and devastating.

When it was finished, my mom took my hand and whispered a Catholic prayer of mourning in my ear. I am forever grateful for the ways that my family accepted me as a gay man, celebrated Howard as my husband, and then shared my grief as his widower.

Rabbi David-Seth explained the Jewish tradition of putting two shovels full of dirt onto the grave. We each took a turn—first with the reverse side to represent reluctance, and then with the correct side to symbolize acceptance. I wasn't ready to accept, but I took the cold shovel and completed the ritual with shaking hands.

I stayed behind as the family left the cemetery. I couldn't pull myself away, still in shock. By the time I finally reached the reception, I saw a familiar face leaving.

"I'm glad we didn't miss you," said Dr. Jennifer Ashton. I recognized her from TV and the pictures Howard had sent from her wedding just three months earlier. She was accompanied by her husband and son. "We're so sorry for your loss."

"I'm really sorry that I had to miss your wedding," I told them. "Howard was so proud to be a part of it. He sent me pictures all weekend. It looked incredible."

"Thank you," Dr. Ashton said, echoing that Howard seemed truly happy, and had shown them pictures of us together.

"I have to ask: did you know the significance of butterflies to Howard?"

"No," she replied.

"So what made you ask Howard to send you butterflies?" I asked.

"I don't know, it just popped into my head."

I told Dr. Ashton the story of Howard's mother and the photo he took of the butterfly she'd sent to him.

"That is truly remarkable," she said. "I miss him. He was a great friend."

The next morning my phone buzzed. It was a text from Dr. Ashton.

> Look what was waiting for me back in New York 🦋

Attached was a photo of a large painting that her daughter had bought for her—of butterflies.

I Just Don't Think I'll Ever Get Over You

Traveling back to Los Angeles, I noticed something odd about doors. Each one that I passed through—leaving the hotel, entering the airport, coming home—caused me anxiety. The feeling was so visceral that I couldn't ignore it.

When I finally closed the door of Howard's house behind me, I dropped my bags and sat on the floor, exhausted. The silence of this place was so wrong.

I decided to try writing a song for Howard. Pulling myself off the floor, I took a seat at the Fender Rhodes in the living room. I turned on the amp and fumbled with some blues chords until a melody came out, soon followed by the words:

> *I miss that easy feeling*
> *With you in my day*
> *Made me a believer*
> *You showed me the way*
> *But I've lost that feeling*
> *The doors have been closed*
> *Your love was so easy*
> *It's so hard to let go*

My chest tightened and my eyes watered as I read the words on paper. As cathartic as it felt to let this out of me, it hurt ten times more seeing it in the world. Another indication that the nightmare was real. I wanted to stop. But I had to keep going. Howard told me to use the pain to write. The muse was speaking, and I had to listen.

I looked back to the line about the doors closing on our life together. The endless possibilities for our love had been abruptly locked out, never to be realized.

But what was it about the doors on my journey home? Why had they tormented me each time I passed through?

I Googled "grief and doors," and what came up was a study from my alma mater, of all places. The headline read, "Walking through doorways causes forgetting." It didn't specifically deal with grief, but it referred to doorways as "event boundaries." Each time we pass through a doorway, our minds subconsciously close out the previous location's events and begin anew. It's why we sometimes forget why we entered a room.

It felt like a reasonable explanation for my anxieties. I was reluctant to pass through each door, as it was carrying me farther from Howard. My heart shattered when he passed away in my arms. The fact that my memories of him would inevitably grow hazy turned those fragments to dust. If I just stayed in my room, maybe I could preserve his memory.

The next verse came out as I explored this idea, melted down, pulled myself together, revised, and repeated. Hours later, I had three verses, each of which ended with the refrain, "Your love was so easy, it's so hard to let go."

I played the song from beginning to end a few times. I read the lyrics through tears and sang the words, barely able to catch a breath. By the time I had recorded a satisfactory voice memo of the idea, it was 2:30 a.m. I hadn't left the keyboard for hours, and I realized that my mouth was dry.

As I stood in the kitchen, sipping water and reviewing the recording, it occurred to me that this song didn't have a proper chorus. Did it need one? It didn't have a bridge, either. Did it need one of those? Some of the lyrics seemed too on the nose. Would anyone understand the thing about the doors? Was this song too specific? Did I care? Who was I writing this for?

I refilled my water bottle, my thoughts drifting to a memory of Howard admonishing me for staying up late. He always told me I needed to sleep more. But this song had to be perfect. It was for Howard. I could do better. I turned back to the keyboard.

Then I jumped a foot in the air at a loud noise above me.

The sound was percussive, yet it had a tone to it—like a hollow piece of metal or glass hitting a hard surface and ringing out.

I was startled, but not afraid. The worst thing imaginable had already happened. So I committed the fundamental horror movie mistake and went to investigate.

It sounded like it came from directly above my head, which would be the primary bathroom. I slowly reached in and turned on the light. Nothing on the floor.

I looked in the shower and saw something shiny next to the drain, reflecting the light from overhead.

I shook my head and laughed.

"Hi Howard," I said. "Are you telling me your song is done?"

I squatted down and picked up a metal showerhead attachment. Tears came to my eyes—the first time I'd ever gotten misty while holding this... thing... that gay men use to, um... prepare for sex.

Anyway.

There was no open window, no draft, no air conditioning, nothing that could have rolled this object off the shelf.

A lot of people might insist that the signs Howard sent me on my travels were merely coincidences. But there were so many—and this one was too perfect.

Howard wouldn't drop books to communicate like in *Interstellar*. Of course not. Instead, he nudged a douche nozzle off the ledge in our shower to show me he was still with me.

Oh How Lucky

"Thanks for loving me"

People have never grieved the way we do in the modern digital age.

The moment I had feared arrived sooner than anticipated. It was the moment that I couldn't hear Howard's voice in my head. As much as I tried, it didn't sound like him.

Then I opened my voicemail app. I still had ten of his voicemails saved. My favorite was: "It's very Stevie Wonder of me, but I'm just calling to say I love you."

I downloaded them to my phone and created a playlist. At first, I cried whenever I listened. The torturous part was knowing that I could never oblige his request to call him back.

But I quickly stopped resenting the futility of these messages and just listened to his voice. I savored my little audio snapshot of Howard and counted myself lucky to have recordings of him telling me, "I love you."

I also combed through our photos. There were tragically few to sift through. We had less than one year together so we only got to commemorate one of each holiday.

One Fourth of July, one Passover, one Halloween, one Thanksgiving, one Hanukkah, one Christmas, one New Year's Eve. One birthday for me. One birthday for him—although it wasn't technically his birthday, it was a two-thirds-of-a-hundred party. Looking back, I'm grateful that I put it together or I never would've gotten to see him blow out birthday candles.

Within a few hours I had created a folder with every photo I'd ever taken while we were together. Picking up Howard's phone I did the same, then merged them into my album.

While on his phone I noticed that Howard had also saved several of my voicemails. He kept the one where I first sang "The Best" to him. He saved ramblings from my late-night drives after gigs. And he saved little ditties that I had written for him, partial songs with cute lyrics that I never intended to turn into real songs but wanted him to have. He kept all of them, just as he kept all the cards I sent to him in a box by his desk, right next to a frame in which he rotated his favorite photos of me.

I had been carrying around a matching frame. Mine held a photo of us at the piano playing "Moon River" together—my most precious musical moment. It occurred to me that I might not want to burn out on that memory, so I printed my favorite photos to rotate as he did.

As I pored over our new photo album to make selections for my frame, I realized that a lot of them were motion photos. Tapping and holding the pictures made them move, as the camera recorded a short video before and after the shutter was pressed. It was a highlight reel of our love. I smiled, letting happy tears fill my eyes while I saved these clips as videos.

And then I realized that I could hear him in some of these clips. The motion photos recorded audio! I chuckled at him pointing to the screen and telling me, "You're not getting enough of the scenery." My ten voicemails weren't the only way I could hear Howard talk to me. We didn't have many videos, but we had a lot of these motion photos.

I went through my new photo album and listened to every motion photo, saving more video clips whenever I could hear his voice. Most were trivial. The photos I'd taken of furniture we were considering for our rental in Nashville featured mundane quotes like, "If we move the couch up a couple inches this will fit." But that's all I needed—it was the Howard I loved. Not the one from TV interviews, but the casual one. My best friend. And best friends aren't made of Hallmark movie moments or front-page headline news. They're made day in and day out, through good times and bad. They help celebrate the little wins and they stay during the "hangry" moments.

Friends and family from both sides reached out to me in the days that followed Howard's passing. I discovered that almost everyone carries grief with them but rarely brings it up, unless to comfort someone who has just begun their own journey of grieving. It's a club that none of us wanted to join. Once we're in it, we share an unfortunate but strong bond.

From these discussions I learned that there are many approaches to grieving in this digital age.

For some, it is too painful to watch videos—but sifting through photos brings them comfort. Others have a hard time seeing any images whatsoever. This changes over time. Grief constantly evolves, although it never fully goes away.

I began my personal grief journey by surrounding myself with Howard in as many ways as possible. We had such a short time together that I needed more. Whenever his friends invited me for a meal, I accepted. I wanted to hear their Howard stories. In an Excel sheet I wrote down the anecdotes, the words of wisdom he'd shared with them, and the little synchronicities that I'd been noticing.

Then I printed out our entire text thread.

Each night for several hours I systematically took screenshots of our message history on my phone. I scrolled all the way up to the top, where I first said:

> Mike Maimone

I tackled this project over the course of several weeks. Looking back, we gushed like schoolboys, so transparently in love with one another. But it had come and gone so fast. The question, "Did this really happen?" constantly plagued my brain. This excruciating task helped me verify that yes, we did have a magical year together.

I pressed on, terrified of how I'd feel if I lost all of this. I knew that in time my memories would fade. I had to preserve this journal of our short time together.

While I worked on that project, I also followed along on my Google Calendar. I noted the days that we'd been together in the same place. It came out to a little over half the year in person, even though it took us over two months to meet for the first time. We had worked hard at bridging the gap between Tennessee and California.

I then realized Google had been following us the whole time; I had location tracking enabled on my phone.

At first I thought it was creepy—Google had documented my every move, even drawing a line on a map connecting everywhere I'd been. It was so detailed: light blue for walking, dark blue for driving, and a black arc for flights.

Then I realized what a blessing this was. I could retrace each step I took with Howard. I checked Google Street View to remind myself of every restaurant we ate at, every store we visited, every route we walked. One by one I took screenshots of the days that we spent together. It returned definition to the memories whose edges had already fallen out of focus.

We did so much together in such a short time, I wanted to preserve each moment for as long as possible. Thanks to the otherwise creepy technology, I rewound and remembered even the most ordinary moments we shared, which in retrospect were all significant.

Never before has grief looked like this. In our digital age, we can document everything we do and hold the memories closely.

Of course, it's still not the person.

That's why some people understandably opt out of it. The texts, voicemails, pictures, videos, map points—even Amazon shopping history—they did not constitute Howard.

And neither did his social media. But Howard's story continued after he passed away, so I took to Facebook to share it with his family and friends.

He was mentioned in the "In Memoriam" section at the Emmys. His obituary was published in *The New York Times* and around the world. He received a lifetime achievement award from the Television Publicity Executives Committee. He appeared in a documentary called *Commitment to Life* about the fight against the AIDS epidemic that aired on Peacock and MSNBC. His alma mater Michigan beat arch rival Ohio State and went on to win the national championship.

I posted these updates to Howard's Facebook page on the eleventh of each month after his passing. It became part of my grieving ritual, along with lighting the yahrzeit candle. From the comments, I learned the Jewish saying, "May his memory be a blessing." This beautiful sentiment became my mantra as I gathered all the Howard stories I could find.

I became a custodian of affection for the man who meant so much to so many, and cherished each new story from friends, family, and his entertainment industry colleagues. Soon I'd composed a treatment for a documentary about the boy from Flint who grew up feeling like a "Martian," yet became a pillar of the LGBTQ+ community, famed publicist, and beloved Hollywood luminary.

This next part will sound name-droppy and my inner punk rocker is cringing in anticipation. But as a kid from a small town in Ohio, it was unfathomable that so many famous people took the time to communicate with me. It reflected how much deeper than Hollywood—where I'd heard many people only reach out when they want something—Howard's friendships went. And it showed that genuine people gravitate toward one another in the industry. Don Lemon, Dr. Ashton, Sam Jay, and Melissa Rivers are among the celebrities Howard introduced me to who could have easily lost my number, but didn't.

It was even more surreal to hear from public figures I'd never met but knew from TV and beyond, beginning with the beautiful message from Oprah. Soon after that, Ricki Lake invited me for coffee, shared how much her friend Howard had meant to her, and offered her perspective on grief. And when it came to Howard's documentary treatment and tribute shows, I was stunned to hear back from George Stephanopoulos, Gayle King, Robin Roberts, Ted Braun, and Randy Barbato of World of Wonder, among others.

As an independent artist, I've sent thousands of emails into the void, never to hear a reply. The response from Howard's network was another indication that he had changed my life forever.

The most enduring and articulate responses weren't words at all—it was what people did.

I had lost a lot of weight from not eating. Friends from back east sent me Grubhub. My neighbors dropped off baked goods. Some of Howard's closest friends invited me over regularly for family meals. I carried on Howard's tradition of hosting gatherings at our home, and his friends and family showed up to share stories and Arnold Palmer toasts in his honor.

And some went very far out of their way to just be with me. My mom can't fly for medical reasons, so my parents drove all the way to Michigan from North Carolina to join me and Howard's family at his funeral. My sister also came to Flint, then to L.A. to be with me at Howard's celebration of life and help me settle into my new home. Friends from Chicago flew in to be by my side, too. Those were tremendous displays of love and support that I will never forget.

Through the Changes
"I found my voice"

The week of Howard's memorial in L.A., I headed to our barber at the Hide Room in Burbank. We always went together, and the owner, Angel, would give us back-to-back haircuts and beard trims.

As I drove, I reviewed the playlist I had put together for Howard's celebration of life reception. It needed to represent his musical taste. I added several hits from Stevie Wonder, the Rat Pack, half of *Magical Mystery Tour*—Howard's favorite Beatles record—and several tracks from Steely Dan (after being forced to listen to them, they were starting to grow on me).

My phone rang. It was Stevie Wonder's manager. I gasped. My heart leapt.

"Hello?" I answered.

I was greeted by the sound of an acoustic guitar. Or at least I thought it was an acoustic guitar. It was playing chords, bending from one to the next like I'd never heard before. The progression sounded familiar, but I couldn't put my finger on it.

"Them that's got shall get…" I heard Stevie Wonder sing in his unmistakable voice. I started to tremble. I spotted an empty parking space and swerved into it.

> *Them that's not shall lose*
> *So the Bible said and it still is news*

I started to cry. This was unreal. At the other end of this phone, Stevie Wonder was singing "God Bless the Child."

> *Mama may have,*
> *Papa may have,*
> *But God bless the child that's got his own*
> *That's got his own*

He played the first two verses and then said, "I want to do this with my band, and have you on keys."

He kept playing the chords as he spoke.

"You want me to play keys with you?" I stammered.

"Yeah, we'll run through it," he said, "just talk to my manager and she'll let you know where to go."

"That's amazing, thank you so much," I said. "What key?"

"Let's do it in G#," he answered. I winced. I was bad at improvising in G#.

"Could we do it in G?" I asked. I immediately second-guessed myself. Who asks Stevie Wonder to change the key of a song?

I heard him move the chords down a half-step.

"We could try it," he answered.

We hung up, and I floated all the way to the barbershop.

When I walked in alone, Angel looked puzzled.

I told him that Howard had passed away. He was shocked.

"I'm so sorry," he said. "He was a great man."

While he trimmed my hair, Angel told me he loved that Howard always asked him how his business was doing and even offered to help him.

"Yeah," I sighed. "That's Howard. He loved helping people."

I tilted my head back so Angel could shape my beard. I stopped talking to avoid messing him up. My mind drifted to when Howard and I took turns in this chair. After our mustaches were both trimmed, our kisses got even better—without any hair in the way, our lips made a tighter seal. I thought, *I'd give anything for one more kiss…*

POP!

I jumped at the noise from overhead. It startled Angel, too. It took me a second to realize why it had suddenly gotten darker.

The light bulb above the barber's chair had just popped.

"Hi Howard," Angel said with a smile.

"Wow," I said, stunned.

"Wow!" I repeated. "Unbelievable. Hi Howard."

Feeling like anything was possible thanks to Howard's magic, I went home and called Scott Mauro to relay that Stevie Wonder wanted me to play with his band. Scott was an accomplished producer, one of Howard's longtime friends, and in charge of the celebration of Howard's life. We met in the hospital, but it felt like I'd already known him through Howard's stories and overhearing the two of them on the phone. It was surreal speaking to him now in Howard's absence. I shared the good news.

"That's great, Mike," Scott replied. "Unfortunately, it's going to add too much to the budget. Stevie needs to perform solo."

My heart sank. Scott was doing an incredible job of planning the service. He reminded me of Howard in the way he could solicit the answer he wanted, even when it seemed out of reach. They shared the type of confidence that comes from decades of successfully pulling off spectacular events. I would've been lost if this were up to me.

So when Scott said no, I assumed I had to tell Stevie Wonder we couldn't make it happen. But something clicked inside me.

"How much would it add?" I asked.

"Several thousand dollars," Scott replied. He detailed the additional PA equipment, musical gear, staff, and stage requirements.

"I mean, I know local musicians; we can borrow instruments so we don't have to pay for backline."

We went back and forth for a few days, and eventually Scott made the full band performance happen. But one more issue arose in our final meeting.

I sat at a conference table with Scott, his staff, Stevie Wonder's assistants, and the venue contacts as we went over the logistics one last time. My head swirled with how many moving parts went into this event. From catering to valet to security to the guest list, there were so many variables that I hadn't considered. I was relieved for Scott's expertise. This was going to be a celebration of life that Howard would be proud of.

Then he presented his draft of the program.

I was listed in the middle of the lineup. Howard's celebration of life was to end with a video tribute that Scott prepared and then a performance by Stevie Wonder and his band.

"Scott," I said. "Howard asked me to play last."

The room was silent. I felt all eyes on me.

"I know," he replied. "But that was before we knew that Stevie would have his band with him. It'll just feel like a huge drop in energy if we go from him with his band to a solo performance."

I didn't want to sound entitled. I didn't want to make this about me. I didn't even want to follow the legendary Stevie Wonder. But it's what Howard envisioned. Even after I told him he was crazy, he insisted. I vividly remembered his firmness from our conversation in the hospital. Howard told me I had to. So I had to.

"I'm sorry," I said slowly, "but maybe you could change it up so I don't go directly after Stevie."

Scott reviewed his lineup. It really was almost perfect. He even told everyone to keep their remarks to two minutes, knowing that they would end up speaking for five, which would keep us right on schedule for a tight show. But that was it—he was thinking about it as a show.

"It's not a music festival," I continued. "It's a memorial. And I think that Howard's wishes are the most important. I know he trusted you, and put you in charge, but he told me he wanted his husband to give him his last tribute."

Scott considered it.

"Okay," he said after a moment. "I'll rework the lineup."

As we left the meeting and walked across the beautiful grounds of The Garland, the midday sun peeked between low gray clouds. It was the end of February, and the air was crisp. Then I noticed a snowflake falling in front of me.

"It's snowing!" I heard someone say.

We all looked up.

"Looks like Howard's sending us a little bit of Flint in California," Scott said.

Snowflakes caught the sunshine as they drifted from the sky. Soon there was a flurry of them, melting as they touched the pavement.

"Hi Howard," I said quietly. "Thanks for your help."

There was just one more day until our celebration of Howard's life. I had been practicing my song and Stevie's song for hours all week. I learned "God Bless the Child" in G# and G, just in case. My sister was staying with me, and she said she didn't mind hearing the same two songs on loop.

"I'm heading out to rehearse with Stevie Wonder," I told her as I tied my shoes. She looked at me and smiled.

"I bet you never thought you'd say those words," she said.

"Absolutely not," I said. I took a deep breath. The about-to-be-a-trainwreck feeling was creeping up. Tears filled my eyes. My sister sat next to me. She didn't say anything, letting me work through it.

"I don't think I can do this," I finally said.

"The memorial? You've played a million shows, you'll be fine."

"Yeah, no, I mean… I just mean in general." My self-destructive brain was trying to sabotage me. "We only had a year together. I don't deserve this place."

My sister put a hand on my shoulder and said, "Mike, he wasn't thinking about the time you had. He was thinking about forever. It was already both of yours."

I cried harder, knowing she cared, and that she was right.

When I walked into Stevie Wonder's studio, his rhythm section was already in the live room. His assistant showed me through the control room and out to meet the band. The studio was a keyboard player's paradise, with countless pianos, organs, and synthesizers.

A decade earlier while on tour in the U.K., I had gotten to see Abbey Road and play the riff from "Lady Madonna" on the piano it was recorded on. That live room was massive, capable of housing a full orchestra. This room felt just as big.

The assistant read my mind.

"No videos," he said before leaving the room.

After a few minutes, Stevie Wonder entered the studio, led by his assistant. It was surreal. I looked to the bassist and drummer, who of course weren't freaking out. They played with Stevie all the time. But I suddenly got nervous. One of my musical heroes was walking toward me. He reached out his hand and I shook it.

"Thank you for having me," I said.

"Of course," he replied. "Howard was a great friend."

He sat at the piano, but instead of playing it, he turned to a stringed instrument on a stand next to the piano bench. It looked like a very wide guitar fretboard, only there were piano keys painted where frets would be.

Stevie started to play it, sliding his fingers up and down the strings in different shapes. It sounded like an acoustic guitar. It was the mystery instrument he'd been playing over the phone!

"What's that?" I asked.

"It's called a harpejji," he said. He told me about the instrument, that he was working with the manufacturer to customize it for him.

I sat on the next bench over to play a Wurlitzer electric piano. Stevie swiveled on his bench and started to play a funky riff on the piano. The rhythm section joined in, and we started to warm up together. I did my best to listen and fit in.

When it was time to rehearse "God Bless the Child," Stevie turned again to the harpejji, so his back was to me.

Looking over as we played, there was Stevie Wonder, just a few feet away, singing this beautiful song. I looked closer at the back of his sweatshirt. On it was embroidered a butterfly. I could practically feel Howard there, telling me I was exactly where I was supposed to be.

We ran through the song twice and then jammed for a while. Eventually the drummer, Stanley Randolph, had to leave for another gig. Everyone else headed into the control room and I followed.

Stevie asked the bassist, Brandon Brown, to play some of his own songs through the monitors. They talked for a bit, then Stevie turned away to discuss something on the phone. Brandon and I started talking about his band. When his song finished, I asked him if I could play him one of mine. He put on "Through the Changes." It was Howard's favorite.

After the first chorus, Stevie looked up from what he was doing.

"You sound like the Black Willie Nelson," he said.

"That's Mike," said Brandon.

"Oh," said Stevie Wonder. "Cool voice."

I wanted to run out of the studio and scream to the heavens, "STEVIE WONDER THINKS MY VOICE IS COOL!"

I wanted to find every critical social media comment saying that I couldn't sing and reply, "STEVIE WONDER THINKS MY VOICE IS COOL!"

And I wanted to tell Howard. I wanted to call him and say thanks for putting me in a room with a living legend and my musical hero. I was so happy. I was so proud. And I was so sad.

God Bless the Child

The next day was Howard's memorial. I arrived early and surveyed the venue—Beverly Park at The Garland. It was beautiful, and every one of the five hundred seats would be filled with people who loved Howard. I also set up a camera for livestreaming to those who could not attend in person. My parents and Auntie Liz texted to let me know they were watching and there with me in spirit.

After many hugs and tears, I took my seat in the second row on the center aisle. On my lap I held the photo of Howard and me playing "Moon River" and the celebration of life program. One of my favorite pictures graced the cover—the one I had taken at the Grand Canyon. The same one I'd looked at to get the right vocal take of "The Best." I would need its help again in a few moments.

My sister sat next to me just as she had at Howard's funeral. Eshanthika, who had traveled from Chicago, sat at the other end of our row in front of the podium, ready to film in case the livestream cut out.

Rabbi David-Seth opened the ceremony. He said Howard would want us to remember that although life is sometimes unfair and cruel, we cannot let that stop us from making it count while we're here.

Melissa Rivers moved the audience from tears to laughter. Howard's nephews paid heartwarming personal tributes to their uncle. His brother shared memories from their youth. Dr. Gary and Scott Mauro saluted their friend and colleague. Don Lemon gave a touching speech, saying Howard helped him realize that his personal coming out journey would benefit the entire LGBTQ+ community. Lorna Luft filled in for k.d. lang, who sent her condolences. I played keys with Stevie Wonder on a beautiful performance of "God Bless the Child." He introduced the song with own personal tribute to Howard.

The theme of "guidance" came up in every speech. Howard's light lit the path out of so many people's darkest days.

It all passed in a blur.

But Lizzy's speech will stick with me forever. Toward the end of it, she put my role in Howard's life into a context that I hadn't realized. She said that after Howard's divorce, he paraded around with young men in their twenties, trying to convince everyone that he was happy living the bachelor life.

I thought back to our first correspondence.

He had reached out to me on February 24, 2022—his birthday.

What was he doing chatting up guys on Scruff on his birthday? Howard could have any guy he wanted, and he apparently had several of them after his divorce.

But he was still lonely. What he really wanted was an equal, someone who stimulated and challenged him. He had everything in the world except his soulmate. He was looking for bashert—and he told his friend Rick as much at his birthday dinner. He put it into the universe that the only thing missing in his life was his one true love. He manifested it. I wondered if he was thinking about our Scruff chat earlier in the day—maybe he specifically manifested me.

Lizzy concluded that my presence didn't change Howard so much as smooth his sharp edges, allowing him to connect more deeply with her and others in his life.

My stomach was in knots by the time the video montage ended. I could barely get through Howard's song without breaking down as I practiced in a room by myself. How would I be able to do this in front of several hundred people?

Just as he had done for each speaker, Scott took the podium to introduce me. He had glowing remarks for each of Howard's family members, friends, and former clients who spoke. He gushed over Lorna Luft and Stevie Wonder for lending their time and talent to the ceremony. I wondered what he had to say about me.

"To end," he began, "Howard wanted this, his husband Mike is going to play a song for you."

Eshanthika leaned to look down the aisle at me and mouthed the words, "What the fuck?"

I shrugged. The audience applauded politely as I got out of my seat. The intro was so short it caught me by surprise, and it seemed to take forever to make my way back to the stage, set Howard's photo next to the keyboard, and take my seat.

I looked at the audience, wondering what they thought of me. Scott had just given an introduction fitting of a house boy with a cute little music hobby. No mention of Howard's love and respect for me, or his pride in marrying a man who figured out how to make a living in a cutthroat industry for nearly twenty years, with accomplishments like having played at Lollapalooza, on late night TV, having songs in film and TV, having done theatre tours with huge bands. Nothing like, "Howard was so proud that he would always share his husband's music with his friends and family, and so it's fitting that he requested Mike to close out his celebration of life with his favorite song."

My intro writes itself. But I got none of it.

It felt like he had said, "I planned this incredible celebration of life, but this wasn't my call so if this last guy sucks, it's not on me."

I took a deep breath and vowed that I would get through this song and prove to everyone that I was worthy of Howard's pride. I shoved my prepared notes into my pocket and began to play the chords while sharing that Howard would forever be my muse. But first, I would play his request, my cover of "The Best."

I started the song:

I call you when I need you, my heart's on fire.

My voice surprisingly did not waver. I felt confident. I felt worthy. I felt like I was doing exactly what Howard wanted me to do.

You're simply the best
Better than all the rest
Better than anyone
Anyone I'd ever met

The third verse caused me to stumble briefly:

Oh as long as I'm here in your arms
There's no place I'd rather be.

My voice trembled as I thought of Howard's giant hugs. I realized I'd never feel that safe and warm again.

I took a slightly longer pause before the next chorus, composed myself, and finished the song. As I held the last chord, I lost it.

My legs shook and my hands trembled as I retrieved my framed photo. The tears poured immediately, and I slowly left the stage. I could hear people applauding, but all I could think about was that my monumental task was over, and I had no idea how or why to move forward now. I felt empty. Hopeless. Pointless.

After the memorial, once the guests had mostly cleared out, Scott pulled me aside.

"You were right," he said, hand on my shoulder. "That was beautiful. Absolutely beautiful. It's the way it had to end."

"Thank you," I said. "Great work on everything."

"And we finished right on time," he concluded. "Give everyone two minutes to speak, because you know they'll take five!"

His brief introduction for me was just to keep us on schedule. I had no hard feelings. I needed that chip on my shoulder to get me through the song, and Scott provided it. He was grieving the loss of his close friend and still managed to put together a remarkable event for my remarkable man.

I also owed him a thank you for helping me realize that Howard had changed me.

Over nearly twenty years as an independent musician I'd learned to go with the flow by default. The demanding studio guy doesn't get a callback for session work. The high maintenance indie band doesn't have many friends on the road. The picky hired gun doesn't get invited on the next tour.

It's not a bad thing, in fact, being adaptable comes in handy.

But it did train me to not make a fuss. To subvert myself in the name of the team. Maybe it started as far back as being an offensive lineman in football, a practice player in basketball, a defenseman in lacrosse—come to think of it I was never in a position that got the glory in sports. And then I went into accounting, to be the guy behind the scenes keeping an eye on the books. Then I became a session keyboard player, and then started a band because I didn't think I deserved my own name on the marquee. I had finally started my own solo project when the pandemic hit, I developed a heart condition and canceled my album release tour. I thought I'd be a side man for life.

But I had always dreamed of having more. I wanted to carry the ball. I wanted to be the front man. Howard saw in me star potential when I didn't. Finally, I was starting to believe him.

To be out front you have to be more than visible, more than confident. You have to be outspoken.

Howard showed me that if your intentions are pure and you express your ideas with respect and empathy, you can say whatever you need to say to anyone, even if they don't want to hear it. He didn't care what anyone thought of him. In the end, whoever he was working with—no matter how established and successful—usually ended up saying, "You were right."

Butterfly

*"I'll pour you a cup at coffee time
and say hi when you wave to me with a butterfly"*

54

After eight months the pain hadn't stopped, but it had evolved. It became more like a sustained bass note than a pounding drum solo. Always present, but not as likely to derail my entire day.

By adopting rituals into my daily routine, I learned to work with the grief rather than letting it sabotage me at random. Every morning I woke up and said, "Good morning I love you Howard," kissing his photo on my nightstand. Once downstairs, I poured two cups of coffee and placed one in front of Howard's kitchen counter photo. And then I thanked him for loving me, for looking after me, and for encouraging me to turn our story into art.

I didn't get the standard marriage "obligations and responsibilities" that our wedding officiant Mike Bonin mentioned. Mine were more unusual ones—telling my late husband's story through words and music.

I spent much of the first several months crumpled in a ball under the piano in my studio, crying in between takes of "Moon River," "A Song for You," and the other tracks on an album of covers. Music brings out emotion like nothing else, and the recording of it—trying to capture one perfect snapshot of a song—was brutal.

But in a way, it was also comforting. The grief meant that there was a lot of love left inside of me. An endless supply.

I called the album *Borrowed Tunes, vol. 2: Songs for You*. Original songs would take a long time to produce, so making my second covers record one dedicated entirely to Howard gave me an immediate musical outlet for my grief. I booked album release shows in L.A., New York, and Chicago, pledging the proceeds to the Trevor Project—an organization that provides suicide prevention support for LGBTQ+ individuals.

This wasn't going to be a typical show for me. It was a one-man act in which I would take attendees through my beautiful and tragic year with Howard via these cover songs, telling the stories of why they meant something to us. The final show would be recorded, so that our stories could be released to the world.

As the first show approached, my anxiety mounted. Rehearsals became more and more grueling as I second-guessed my ability to get through the repertoire, much less put on the show that Howard deserved. I spent more time crying on the floor of my studio.

Then I got a message that snapped me into reality.

It was from an acquaintance of Howard's named Scott Schwimer, who had sadly lost his husband Michael nearly two years prior. He said that Howard had messaged him his condolences via Facebook—but he hadn't received it until just now. Facebook emailed him out of the blue saying he had an unread message from Howard Bragman.

After reading Howard's message, Scott saw my monthly updates for Howard's friends and family. He then composed his own message of condolences for me.

His words resonated. It was clear that he understood what I was going through. Losing our best friends and forever guys was "like being cut off at the knees."

He said that a change of scenery had helped him during his first summer and offered up the spare apartment at his rental in Laguna Beach if I wanted to get away. I asked if I could bring a small keyboard and rehearse for my tour, and he said yes.

The night I arrived, I set up my keyboard on the back deck. It was dark, so I faced inside and let the living room lights illuminate the keys. I took a deep breath and smelled sea air. I heard crashing waves below. I immediately felt more relaxed than I had in my studio. Scott said he'd give me some privacy and took his dog for a walk.

I started with "The Best." As I played, I noticed the lights above the mantel pulsing slowly.

That's odd, I thought. *They weren't doing that before.*

I stopped playing.

The lights stopped pulsing.

I started playing.

The lights started pulsing.

It wasn't like the flicker of a spotty connection. It looked more like someone playing with a dimmer switch. The lights faded smoothly from off to on and back.

I smiled at the thought…

"Howard?" I asked, stopping the song. The lights came on full brightness for just a moment and then went out.

I got my camera out and hit record, placing it on my lap facing the ceiling. I continued the song.

The lights resumed their dance as I sang. They appeared to be in rhythm with my singing, only just a hair behind. As if the first word of each line were a clue to the rest of the lyric. I shook my head.

"Hi Howard," I said aloud. "You have such a unique way of singing along."

Scott returned from his walk.

"Scott, have your lights ever done this before?" I asked.

"Done what?" he said, not knowing where to look.

I nodded inside. "That."

I resumed singing, and the lights resumed their dance.

"No!" he said in awe.

I kept playing, and the lights kept pulsing, gently, seemingly in agreement with my lyrics. They kept going as I practiced my entire set. Finally, I had to stop. And so did the lights.

GUESS WHAT? I LOVE YOU

When Howard's tribute shows and unveiling were over, I returned to our empty home, clung to my lummox and cried in our bed.

I felt drained. It had been such an emotional journey. I wanted to sleep for days.

But one of Howard's former colleagues, Will Armstrong, had invited me to tag along with his husband and a group of ten of their friends to Puerto Vallarta. I had accepted the invitation, thinking it would be healthy to relax after my tribute tour. But the time was now here, and I didn't want to leave. I was supposed to visit Mexico with Howard. It felt wrong to go without him.

I had also overwhelmed myself with outlets for my new creative purpose—telling Howard's story.

I was pitching a documentary about Howard's life and impact on the LGBTQ+ community. I'd started writing songs for an album inspired by him. I was taking acting classes—Howard had always said the camera loved me in my music videos. And I'd started this, my first book. I was trying everything I could to keep busy, to use the pain for creativity in hopes it wouldn't consume me.

I needed a roadmap, or nothing would get finished. I got out a sheet of paper and made three column headings to start to-do lists:

1. *Book / Doc*
2. *My Music*
3. *Acting*

I figured I would call Will, apologize, and tell him that I couldn't make it. Then I would throw myself back into making art. But I decided to sleep on it.

In the morning, my phone rang. It was Dr. Jennifer Ashton. She was calling from Mexico, with a medium beside her.

"She doesn't know anything about Howard," Dr. Ashton said excitedly. "But she sounds just like him. You have to hear this." I could hear a woman's voice in the background, and Dr. Ashton relayed the messages.

She said he wouldn't normally like the flowers, but in this case they were perfect. This must've been about our wedding flowers—I'd placed them prominently in our living room, thinking there was no way that Howard would approve of fake pastel flowers in his home.

Next, she said that a woman who was like a sister to him needed to speak with me immediately. She said the person had an "A" name. At that moment my phone rang—it was Aunt Manya. In my phone her first name was "Aunt" and her last name was "Manya."

Shocked, I excused myself and took her call.

When I called Dr. Ashton back, the medium was thankfully still there. She told me Howard said, "Focus on job number two, forget about one and three. Does that mean anything to you?"

My jaw dropped. I got out my notepad with the three columns.

Was Howard telling me to focus on my music?

Finally, she told me, "He wants you to go to the beach, wear the swimsuit he got you, meet new friends, don't worry about money, just focus on friendships and health."

I was stunned. Howard had given me a new Speedo for Puerto Vallarta even though he knew I was more of a trunks kind of guy. And he was always worried about me stressing over making ends meet and not sleeping enough—especially with my heart condition.

Could this be Howard telling me chill out and go to Mexico?

I didn't cancel.

On the trip down, I told Will about my tour, about the strange and wonderful coincidences, and I showed him my new tattoo of Howard's initials in the shape of a butterfly on my forearm. He loved the story about Howard getting butterflies from his mom, and then Dr. Ashton getting them from Howard.

"I believe it," Will said. "If anyone could send winged creatures from beyond the grave, it's Howard." He told me how much Howard had meant to him—he'd changed Will's life by getting him into PR.

We arrived at the house—it was an enormous mansion. The massive front doors were wide open for us.

Our group walked in, collectively stunned and staring all around at our luxurious lodging. On the opposite side of the foyer we could see through forty-foot glass doors that opened onto a massive backyard pool, and beyond that, the Pacific Ocean.

I caught Will's eye. He was starting to tear up. He nodded toward the high ceiling. "Look up," he said.

A butterfly circled the entryway, soaring around the high ceiling.

My eyes got misty, too. It was a wave from Howard, telling me this was the right decision. Telling me to enjoy myself. Telling me to keep living my life.

I moved into the next room of the house, trying not to break down in front of the group. In the dining room stood a beautiful grand piano with a shiny black finish.

I walked over and lifted the key cover.

The brand name stared back at me.

I felt my heart skip.

I'd never even heard of this type of piano.

It was a Howard.

I was once an accountant. That part of me thinks, *What are the odds?* That a butterfly would greet us when we arrived. That lights would flicker, a bulb would pop, a shower attachment would fall, at exactly the moments they did. That old friends would keep me company on a flight, or that Stevie Wonder would wear a butterfly sweatshirt on the day of our rehearsal. That a cardinal would peek into the security camera on our Nashville house, causing my phone to buzz with a "person detected" alert during Howard's memorial in Los Angeles. What were the odds that a Howard piano—a company established in Ohio in 1895—would be at my friend's vacation home in Mexico?

As a songwriter and performer, though, I've come to rely less on analytics and more on intuition—like the "Year of Yes" mentality that led me to Howard. So I simply interpret these events as reminders that we're part of something greater than the world we can measure.

Such synchronicities don't give me paranoia anymore; they reassure me that I'm on the right path. And they help me believe that our souls do not cease to exist once our hearts stop beating.

Where do they go? It would be audacious to claim that I know. But I suspect they are in the energy all around us. I think of it as The Light.

I believe that Howard is waiting for me there.

When I see him again, I'll squeeze him tight, losing myself in his great big bear hug like I used to.

Knowing me, I won't be able to hold back as I lament how unfair it was that his incredible life ended too soon, that we had our great love cut short, and how we were cheated out of a lifetime of adventures together.

Of course, Howard will just smile and say, "Guess what?"

I'll roll my eyes and ask, "What?"

And he'll tell me, "I love you."

Acknowledgements

Although much of my life is readily available online, I guard closely the intimate details of my personal relationships. So the concept for this book began far from how it turned out.

As I learned more about my remarkable husband after he passed away, I initially wanted to share his legacy with the world by making a documentary. I searched Howard's contacts for "producer" and reached out to a few. Everyone I approached loved my treatment and encouraged me to keep going with it. Ron Sylvester (*Commitment to Life*) also recommended that since a documentary would take years to fund and complete, in the meantime I should write a book. It would help me capture and preserve the great love of my life before the memories inevitably faded.

Setting pen to paper, I realized I was doing both at once—telling the world about Howard through the lens of our love story. From the outset, it felt like the only way to tackle a book about a man who helped so many live their authentic lives would be to share openly and honestly. I think intimacy serves the narrative. As both a masterful storyteller and willing muse, I'm sure that Howard would agree. I'm also sure he got a good chuckle out of my discomfort with my parents reading the more sexual passages.

Although the writing and editing forced me to revisit the most painful time of my life repeatedly for two and a half years, it also allowed me to revisit the most wonderful and transformative time. I celebrated the ways Howard changed my life and vice versa. It set me on a path of healing. I would not have made it this far on the journey if not for the blessing of many supportive people in my life. My apologies in advance to those of you I have inadvertently left out.

To my sister Lea. As Howard lit the way through many people's darkest days, you did for me. Thank you for being there. I also want to give you credit for giving me the perspective on Howard's memorial not being a "music festival," but I had to condense the planning process for brevity. And thanks for your editing help.

To my Mom and Dad. Thank you for every opportunity growing up, and for giving me the tools to navigate adulthood. You said you wished you could have been there for me in L.A., and I assure you, you were and are.

To Auntie Liz. I'm sorry we share the bond of grief, but your resilience and ability to stay kind and loving to those around you inspired me. I'm grateful for your example.

To Howard's family. Alan, David and Jaclyn, Adam, Aunt Manya, Julie, Lizzy and Tom, Ben, Leslie, David-Seth and Dori, Gaylyn, Shelly, Carol, and everyone else, thank you for welcoming me into the family. It's an honor.

To Ron Sylvester. Thank you for setting me on this path.

To Kyle Fager. Thank you for giving me the confidence that I could write this book. You were the first person I came to for guidance, and I'm grateful that you steered me all the way to the end.

Thanks to my friends who came from near and far to be with me at Howard's memorial: Bob Buckstaff, Annie Prichard, Eshanthika Wijesinha, Melissa Reed, Manny Sanchez, De'Mar Hamilton, Alejandra Gracia, Rob and Natalie Holysz, Josh Siegel, Ashleigh Long, Amber Farris, Pat Amato and the POR family.

To my friends Phillip-Michael Scales, Eduardo Amarel, Ellen Angelico, Doug Cornett, Kristina Cottone, Alex Elman, Kristen Ford, Melisa Freeman, Justin Gibson, Christopher Gold, Daniel Good, Tom Goss, Rob Gould, Nathan Graham, Becca Grischow, Phil Jones, John Krane, John MacNeil, Pat McGarry, Patrick McIsaac, Drew McKechnie, Julian Michael, Nikki Morgan, Matt Padberg, Chris Pagnani, Steve Parola, Ian Phillips, Brendan J. Schneider, DeMark Schulze, Dusty Segretto, Joe Shadid, Ian Tsan, Ed Steinfeld, Chris Van Dunk, Kurt and Matt, Larry and Ray - thanks for reaching out to comfort me, honor Howard, and encourage me to write this story.

To my neighbors Jeff, Erica, Erin and Patrick, as well as Dave Carey, thank you for helping me make a new home when I was feeling lost.

To the Lewinsky Family, Hersh Davis-Nitzberg, Holly & Dorey, Rick Jacobs, John Amaechi, Will Armstrong, Dr. Jennifer Ashton, Ali Axelrad, Steve Baker, Hilary Bibicoff, Ted Braun, Andrew Brettler, Hilda Catota, Alexander Cardinale, Dr. Gary Cohan, Aaron & Dana Colby, Cory Councill, Susan DuBow, Sarah Kate Ellis, Barbara Fedida, Liz Flynt, Susan Haber, Olivia Hill, Sam Jay, Yanise Monet, Peter & Helene Jaycen, John & Gio, Ricki Lake, Andee & Kenny Lee, Don Lemon, Louise Linton, Lorna Luft, Marc & Jay, Christian Martinen, Scott & Harriett Mauro, Jim & Keri Moret, Samual Moscoso, Michael Nyman, Jeanne Phillips, Marv Pollack, David Reddish, Melissa Rivers, Amy Robach & TJ Holmes, Jill Rosenbaum, Barbara Schroeder, Jeffrey Schwarz, Nancy A. Shenker, Bill Silva, Kim Sudhalter, Ryan Tasz and Wouter, Esera Tuaolo, Ned Wallroth, Oprah Winfrey, Cyd Zeigler, Wendy Zocks, and anyone I'm missing from Howard's massive orbit, thank you for inviting me for meals, looking after me, checking in on me, acknowledging me, and/or helping me learn more about my incredible husband.

Thank you to Stevie Wonder and his team for fulfilling one of Howard's last wishes and giving me a musical moment I'll never forget in the process.

Thank you to Alicia Marting, Jesse Beal, and the University of Michigan Spectrum Center for everything you do for the LGBTQ+ community in Ann Arbor and beyond. It means a lot that you've included me and I'm proud to witness Howard's legacy in action.

Thank you to Fran Montano at Actors Workout Studio for helping me embark on a new creative journey. And to my classmates Reilly, Jonah, Kimberly, Sarah, Rachel, Anthony, Parker, Kiana, Jhoana, Amy, Michael, and Joey.

Thanks to the Mexico Adventure crew: Will, Bill, Ethan, Toby, Matt, Kevin, Tucker, Stephan, Nicholas, Miguel, Will, and Cam.

To my AP English teacher Tom Davis, thank you for inspiring me to stay hungry and stay foolish.

To Sister Mary Laurel from Ashtabula Catholic. In eighth grade you told me that if I kept writing, I'd become a published author someday. It took me a while, but I got here. Thanks for encouraging me, I never forgot that vote of confidence.

To Celeste Fine and Ben Kaslow-Zieve at Park, Fine & Brower, thank you for your direction, editing, and guidance in taking this from a first draft to a published book.

And to Scott E. Schwimer. Thank you for your moral support, your professional expertise, your encouragement, and your companionship.

Thanks as always to my Patreon subscribers. I couldn't devote so much time and energy to making art without your support—both financially and emotionally. Thank you for letting me know you're listening, reading, and always encouraging me to keep making more stuff for you to enjoy. In order of appearance: Eshanthika Wijesinha, Ian Phillips, Cristina Amador Perez, Chris Van Dunk, Stephen Parola, Alexandra, Dennis Switt, Jeff Hackbarth, Shawn Poulter, Eric Hurm, Melissa Freeman, Michael Weggeland, Elizabeth Harper, Bryan Batsell, Matt Padberg, James Olski, DeMark Schulze, Lee Nixon, Jason Sharp, Joseph Braun, Brad Wortman, Dave Ebersole, Ryan Wierzba, William Tyler, Joe Truesdale, John Mark Reddish, Sebastian Farchione, Jack Coleman, Robin Roth, Bill Larkin, VanceMan, Jamie O'Neill, Melo, Franklin M. Harrison, John Maimone, Auntie Liz, Justin Williams, Ian Harris, Clarinda Jordan, Chuck, PAG, Al Stout III, Alec Herr, Robert Heinzelman, Heith Rogers, Travis, Sam, Andreas Leja, Lee Lambourne, Lee Blair, Bertrand, Chen Chen, Lucas Campos, Nancy A Shenker, Michael Ruebensam, RaiderRed, Odd-Geir Gundersen, Jeff0908, Bill Hunter, Richard T, Jeffrey Costa, John Wigley, Matthew Gardner, Tonihernsac, Chris Ostapchuk, Matt Stamper, Clifton McReynolds, Tonio Aleman, Shawna, Ray deJongh, Dustin Cushman, Collin McHugh, Jim Pohl, Jared McLaughlin, David

DeWitt, David Dubin, Phil, Jacobus Erasmus, Casey, Jorge Janeiro, Morgan Rumpf, Dave Rossi, Drew McKechnie, Les Siewert, Nicholas Costopoulos, Chris Lewis, Jared Lyon, Matt Colagiuri, Peter Calabrese, Juronimo, Paquito, Alan Robinson, Dan Garcia, Dean Henson, Clemente, Daniel Thelen, Zachary Peachy, Rod Summers, Joe Anderson, Aaron the Baron, Stephen Martin, Nicholas, Joseph Contardo, Daniel Vivacqua, Damian Clancy, Barry Alexander, Ryan Adams, Austin Blake, Patrick Cenci, Jeremiah Nichols, Doug Carpenter, Bailey Klein, Nicholas Baute, Mike Burgess, Paul Mandry, Christophe-Thomas Simmons, Charlie Morse, Jeremy, Jake Lanagan, William McGrath, Tyler Fiore, Michael Glover, Trenton Grace, Marco Campos, J, Alan Westley, Juan Camilo Daza Medina, Todd Taylor, Mike Kukahiwa-Haruno, Thomas O'Handley, Fencon, JDog, Dusty Phillips, Robert Evers, Bobby Evers, Christopher Robinson, Nicholas Morales, Morgan Adams, Martin Zizka, Paul Morbitzer, Kim Ho, Matty B, Brett Jarvis, Terrence Braddock, Don Bigger, Liz Maimone, Tony Jasinski and Ruben Corro, Mario Zertuche, Kevin Van Valkenburg, Georgi Nikolov, Juan Carlos Del Prado Del Aguila, and Bo Powell.

About the Author

Mike Maimone is a singer-songwriter, pianist, and producer whose music and life story are defined by resilience, passion, and authenticity. Growing up in Ashtabula, Ohio, he was an all-state athlete, even playing basketball against LeBron James, while also studying and performing classical piano. After earning a business degree from the University of Notre Dame, he briefly worked as an accountant before leaving the corporate world to pursue music full-time.

He has published over 200 songs as varied as his life experiences, which have been featured in TV, film and on the radio. On top of being a prolific recording artist with over 60 independent releases on his own label, Maimone has averaged over 100 tour dates per year since 2005.

Performing as a solo artist, fronting his trio Mutts, or playing keys for other artists, he has taken the stage at legendary venues across the country, as well as major festivals including Lollapalooza, Sasquatch!, and Riot Fest. Maimone has performed with Stevie Wonder, opened for Blink-182, Weezer, Black Flag, and Imagine Dragons and has toured with OK Go, Plain White T's, Blues Traveler, Murder By Death, and The Hold Steady.

His fifteenth album serves as a companion piece to this, his first book. *Guess What? I Love You* is available on CD, vinyl, and all digital platforms. Find out more at mikemaimone.com.

Howard's memorial video and a selection of his interviews are available at howardbragman.com.